A
STEADFAST
HEART

Gillian Ogilvie

1

Published by Anvil Authors

LA14 3AT

A CIP catalogue record for this book is available from
the British Library

ISBN 978-1-387-18995-3

Cover Art/Graphics by Graham Troth

Steadfast - resolute, unflinching, dependable,
constant, tireless, enduring, faithful, true and loyal

The Oxford Thesaurus

*

In spite of all the questions, mysteries and doubts put into
her mind, Sally would continue to keep faith, wouldn't
she?

*

As Brad said, 'misunderstandings can make big problems
if we let them.'

*

The Elizabethans believed the seat of the affections was
the stomach. Perhaps that is why they ate such enormous
meals – talk of feeding one's love!

Once it was realised that, by pumping blood round the
body, it was the heart that kept us alive, Romantics
moved the seat of affections to this indispensable organ.

*

Also by Gillian Ogilvie

<u>Novels</u>

Lost in France
Broken Wings
Living without Lucy
Homecoming
Dragonfly Crossroads
Connections   Book One   Entrapment
              Book Two   Still Waters
Connections   Book Three   Sins of the Fathers
Connections   Book Four   Onward and Upward
The Triple Braid

<u>Murder Mysteries</u>

Murders like Buses
Murders like Pyramids
Murders like Vengeance
Murders like Traffic Lights

<u>Non-Fiction</u>
Shared Thoughts on Random Themes
More Shared thoughts on Random Themes

4

A STEADFAST HEART

Chapter One

'Look, Sally! This is for you.' Five-year-old Lucy held up the completed daisy chain for inspection.

'It's lovely, darling. Thank you.' Sally Fletcher gracefully leaned over and lowered her head to let Lucy hang the chain around her neck.

Bradney Picton was treated to the sight of a pair of long, lightly tanned legs rising from scuffed trainers, curving deliciously up and up to disappear into tight, faded denim shorts, very short shorts.

In spite of his bad mood, Brad's lips twitched in an appreciative smile. He lingered for a while to admire the view then, as the owner of the legs straightened up, he moved away and she was soon hidden by the trees.

He had hoped some exercise in the fresh air would rid him of the restlessness which plagued him. He felt caged by the walls of the Gate Lodge and he always thought better on the move. While he walked through the Home Park he could calculate just which trees would need to be felled. He strode on deep in thought.

'Howzat!'

Philip's excited young voice rang out. Sally laughed.

'Well and truly caught. OK! I'm out. Here's the bat. Where's Lucy? I thought she was fielding.'

'She's making more soppy daisy chains,' answered seven-year-old Philip with all the scorn of an older brother. 'She's a useless fielder anyway. I promise I won't hit it too far for you to run, Sally.'

'Thank you, dear. You know how old and decrepit I am these days,' she answered, stooping over with a hand to her hip in caricature of an old crone.

Philip grinned, unrepentant, and took up his position. He held the bat in front of the stumps which were his pride and joy. Dad had made them for him. 'Middle and leg,' he announced solemnly.

'Middle and leg,' agreed Sally, not having the faintest idea what it meant, but quite happy to go along with the ritual. She bowled the tennis ball overarm to him. His young male pride would have been wounded had she lobbed him a gentle underarm ball. Philip stepped forward and swung his bat. There was a satisfying 'thunk' as the wood made contact with the ball, which sailed past Sally's left ear.

'Well done, Philip,' she exclaimed and turned to race after it. 'Oh! No! Lookout!' she shouted as a figure appeared between the trees in the direct path of the ball's flight.

Too late. The ball hit the man a glancing blow on the cheek. He put his hand to his head and staggered back.

Sally ran forward. 'I'm so sorry,' she cried. 'Are you alright?'

The stranger looked dazed, as though he didn't know what had happened.

'We had no idea anyone was about,' explained Sally.

The man looked around, taking in the scared face of Philip still holding the bat, Lucy looking up with interest from her daisy chain, and the ball which lay at his feet. He glared at Sally.

6

'Are you in charge of these children?' he barked.

'Yes.'

'Well, in future I suggest you keep them under better control. Assault is a very serious crime.'

'Hang on a minute.' Not for nothing was Sally's rich brown hair shot through with fiery red highlights. 'I've said I'm sorry, but you stepped out of the trees with no warning. You should have been looking where you were going. No-one comes to this part of Home Park these days. As it is, you were at the end of the ball's flight, so it can't have hit you too hard.'

Brad wasn't used to people answering him back. His mouth set in a firm line. His nostrils looked pinched as cold grey eyes bored into Sally's.

'What do you mean, no-one comes to this part of the Park these days?'

'Since old Mrs Masterson died three years ago, the Hall has been empty. Her visitors used to ride in the Park, and sometimes she used to come this way to the village, but now there's no-one.'

'Don't be too sure. Things could change. And keep those children under control.'

Stunned by these cryptic utterances and the order barked at her, Sally's mouth dropped open. The man turned on his heel and stalked away.

'Are you alright, Sal? He was ever so cross, wasn't he? I'm sorry he shouted at you.' Philip's little brown paw slid into Sally's hand.

She looked down into his pale face. His eyes were big with fright. Just at that moment Lucy started to cry.

'Hey, you two. It's alright. No harm done. Stop crying Lucy. Philip and I are fine. It was just one of those things and it was a good hit Phil, one of your very best.'

A wavering smile crossed the boy's face and Lucy dried her tears.

'Come on then, let's go home. There are fish fingers for tea, and I made jam tarts yesterday. I think there's some ice cream left to have with them,' Sally coaxed the children.

As they gathered up their cardigans and toys, she silently cursed the stranger who had upset them. Over the past eighteen months both children had gradually become more confident, but it didn't take much to put the fearful look back into Philip's eyes. When that happened Lucy always cried. Her older brother's uncertainty communicated itself to her instantly. Sally stifled a sigh and chatted gaily to the children as she led them through the gate in the fence, which separated the cottage garden from the Home Park belonging to the Masterton estate.

As she prepared their tea she couldn't help thinking about the angry man. Who was he? Certainly not a local. She knew everyone within a radius of twenty miles. Even with that frown and his cold grey eyes he was good-looking enough to be a film star. His hair was a deep brown, darker than her own, with one unruly lock flopping over the broad sweep of his forehead. Sally'd be prepared to put money on the annoyance he felt whenever that wave fell across his brow. But to a woman it was very attractive. A delicious shiver ran down Sally's spine, finishing somewhere below her belly-button as she remembered those hard eyes assessing her. And he was tall, at least six feet, with broad shoulders and long, long legs. Sally's personal ideal man in looks would be the actor, Sean Bean, as he portrayed *Sharpe* on the television. She used to have a habit of scoring any new man she met against this icon.

The stranger definitely merited a nine out of ten, perhaps nine and a half?

'Are the fish fingers ready yet, Sal?'

Philip's plaintive voice recalled Sally from her musings. She laughed at herself and gave the children her full attention until they were fed, bathed and ready for bed. Then while Dad read them their stories, she fixed a meal for him and herself.

When her chores were done for the day, Sally's thoughts turned again to the handsome stranger. She lay in bed and relived their meeting. The village could do with an injection of new male blood, but preferably someone with a better temper than Mr Grey Eyes. She flushed as she felt again his cold dismissive glance. If only she hadn't been wearing her ancient shorts. And why did she have to meet a new man when she'd put her heavy curls up in bunches to take their weight off her neck in the heat? It was too bad.

With a slight shock Sally realised this stranger had roused a real interest in her. She seemed to have been alone for such a long time, by her own choice. But she was a healthy young woman and surely window-shopping could do no harm? Even though she now had the house and the children to look after, she could still feel attracted to the opposite sex. Despite the hurt Laurence had inflicted, her life would go on. And the stranger had certainly been a hunk worth daydreaming about. Perhaps he was just passing through? She'd probably never see him again. What had he meant about changes in the Home Park? Sally drifted off to sleep to dream of Philip bowling peas to Grey Eyes who batted them away with an outsize fish finger. He couldn't score any runs because Lucy had wound daisy chains around his legs.

9

At the Gate Lodge, Bradney Picton cursed himself for his inattention, his impatience, and generally for the way in which he had handled himself in the Park. The ball hadn't really hurt him, just taken him by surprise. Unfortunately the whole incident too closely resembled the flashbacks he sometimes suffered at night. Perhaps he wasn't as 'over' that accident on the rig as he thought? He'd snarled a rebuke before thinking straight. Most unlike him.

But that girl had certainly not let him get away with it. He grinned. She had wonderful hazel eyes and daggers of annoyance had lent them attractive sparks. When she grew up, she'd be a real smasher.

How old would she be? Sixteen, seventeen perhaps? Maybe eighteen. Hard to tell really. She wore no make-up and there'd been a flush on her cheeks. Was it the heat or annoyance with him? She was babysitting those children and dressed like a teenager in her shorts with scruffy trainers, and her curly hair up in two bunches. But the figure so well defined by her tight shorts and skimpy T-shirt was all woman. Nothing of the child there.

Mustn't go down that road. He'd never been a cradle-snatcher. The women Brad mixed with were sophisticates who knew the score. Mutual enjoyment and no strings.

The little firecracker had spoken as if she treated the Home Park as an extension of her own garden. Obviously things had got slack since the old lady died. There'd been no-one in charge for nearly three years. All that must change now. The locals must learn they could no longer trespass. The sooner the quack signed Brad off as fit and Farthing got down here and started work the better. Time was passing with nothing getting done, an intolerable state of affairs for a man who liked to push the action along at every level of a project.

Brad fixed himself a microwave dinner while his brain went over the plans he had for the Hall and surrounding estate. Usually he liked to prepare a proper meal, eat off china at a table set with silver and crystal, and enjoy a glass of good wine. The civilised ritual soothed him, reminded him of all he had achieved and underlined a promise he had made to his dead mother. But tonight he was fretting with impatience at his enforced inactivity.

He threw the food cartons in the bin and sat down at his laptop. As the sky grew darker and sounds of life in the village died away, the lights in the Gate Lodge burned through the night.

Chapter Two

'I met a young girl yesterday with a couple of children in tow, a boy and a girl,' Brad remarked casually to the motherly woman behind the counter of the village store.

'That'll be our Sally, Sally Fletcher.'

As he had hoped, Mrs Wilson was only too willing to impart information. He had taken her measure on first arriving in the village and handing in his order for morning papers. When he emerged from a third degree on himself and his reasons for coming to the village it was clear Mrs Wilson liked to know all about everything and everyone in the area. She was not averse to passing on the information to whomsoever was interested.

'A wonderful little mother she is to those poor children,' she went on.

Brad was taken aback. Mother? Surely she wasn't old enough? A gymslip pregnancy perhaps? He sighed. Surely in this day and age, with sex education in schools, this kind of thing shouldn't happen?

'I didn't see a wedding ring. Is she married?'

Mrs Wilson's permed curls bounced around with the force of her indignation.

'No. Poor girl! She was engaged, but when all the trouble happened, he didn't want to know.' She sniffed. 'He went off to America without her. And good riddance I say. That'll be three pounds seventy-five with the honey, please, Mr Picton.'

Brad left the shop and crossed the road. He intended going to the church to wander round the graveyard and take a look at the quaint inscriptions on the old stones. But he paused in his walk to glance at the headlines of his paper, although his thoughts were far away.

Another man who turned out to be a rat. Running away from responsibilities. Just like his own father. His parents had been married, but that hadn't stopped Jake Picton walking out on his wife and seven-year-old son. Brad's stomach tightened and his newspaper was in danger of being irreparably crushed as he remembered the hard years which had followed. Abandoned in a strange town, it had been a desperate struggle for his mother to feed and clothe them both. At least this girl, this Sally, seemed to have people around who would support her. Did she live with her parents? She was obviously local.

As Brad glanced again at the headlines, the bold print stark in the bright sunlight, a pain shot through his head and everything went black.

As Sally swung along the warm pavement her thoughts were busy with her usual domestic tasks. She had washing powder on her list, and it would be nice to get some fresh fish if she caught Dan-the-Van on his rounds. Philip needed new laces in his school shoes, and she mustn't forget the flour for her cake contribution to the Church Fete on Saturday.

She noticed her stranger from the Home Park on the other side of the road. He seemed to be reading his paper but then lifted his head and looked around. Sally waved her hand in friendly greeting, but he ignored her and looked away. Rude man. Well, what did she expect? He'd made his point quite clear yesterday. Sally and the children were a nuisance. She strode on and turned in towards the shop door, but something made her look over her shoulder. Now she was closer, she could see Mr

Angry's face more clearly. Sally stopped abruptly, causing Mary Jones walking behind to bump into her. With a muttered apology Sally stepped back and looked again at the face across the road. She'd made no mistake. The man was afraid. Not just afraid. She saw real terror etched there. Her warm heart went out to him. It didn't matter he had been so nasty to her and the children. Here was someone in need. She hurried across the road.

'Are you alright? Can I help?'

His head swung round in the direction of her voice. 'Who's that? Who are you?'

'I'm Sally Fletcher. We met yesterday in the Home Park.'

'Oh, yes. I remember. You hit me with a ball.' He put his hand to his head as he spoke.

Sally frowned. Did he have a headache? Surely this wasn't a delayed reaction to yesterday's blow on the head? The ball had almost reached the end of its flight.

'Is anything wrong? You seem . . . distressed.'

Again his head turned. He reached both hands out in front of him dropping his newspaper and bag of shopping as he did so.

'Where are you? I can't see. I can't see anything.'

Sally heard the note of panic rising in his voice. She slipped her arm through the handle of her basket and caught the man's hands in both of hers.

'I'm here. Hang on. You're alright. Just try and stay calm and tell me what happened.'

The firm, soothing voice she used with the children when they were upset seemed to steady him. He closed his staring eyes and breathed deeply two or three times.

'Thanks. I'm afraid I've been overdoing it. I'm recuperating from a bang on the head.'

Sally winced and caught her underlip between her teeth. How dreadful he should already have an injury, and then the tennis ball should hit him.

As though he could read her thoughts, he smiled briefly. 'Don't fret. It was nothing to do with your ball. I've been warned to take it easy. In fact, that's why I'm here. But frustration got the better of me last night and I foolishly spent hours at my laptop. This is the result. I can't see a thing.' A hint of panic returned. 'If you could just help me home, I'd be very grateful. Then I'll phone the quack and see what's what.'

'Of course. Where are you staying?'

'At the Gate Lodge.'

'So you're Mr Picton?'

Brad nodded. 'Bradney Picton. You've been talking to Mrs Wilson.'

Sally laughed. 'You've obviously learned she's the local fount of all knowledge. I suppose I should have thought of you when we met yesterday, but . . .' she stopped. How could she say his bad temper had argued against him being the Mr Picton whom Mrs Wilson had described as being so pleasant and friendly? 'I didn't think of it.' She finished lamely.

'If I put my arm over your shoulder, you could put your arm around my waist and warn me of any forthcoming steps or obstacles,' suggested Brad, anxious to get back to the Lodge and phone Peter Harrison, his specialist.

Sally cast a glance across the road. She knew at least three pair of eyes were monitoring her meeting with Bradney Picton. Then she shrugged. It couldn't be helped. She couldn't abandon the man. She stooped to retrieve his belongings, put them in her basket and prepared to become the latest topic for village gossip.

'OK. Here we go.' She slid her free arm around his waist and drew him to her side. If she leaned her head ever so slightly it would fit exactly in the hollow below his collarbone, cradled by his shoulder and the strength of his chest. Sally pulled her errant thoughts back to the job in hand.

'Set off with your left foot and I'll use my right. That way our legs are moving together,' she instructed. 'The pavement is flat and smooth here for about twenty yards. I'll warn you when we have to step down to cross the lane-end.'

'Thank you.'

She could feel the tension in his body as he tried to put his trust in her not to let him stumble or fall. To put him at his ease she chuckled.

'What's the matter?' His sightless eyes turned to look down at her.

'You do realise you've ruined my reputation? Every customer in Mrs Wilson's will go home tonight and tell the world we were embracing in the village street. Steady now,' she added, as suddenly she had to steer him back to the centre of the pavement. 'After that manoeuvre,' she laughed again, 'they'll probably think we're drunk as well.'

The interior of the Gate Lodge was as tidy and impersonal as any hotel room. There were none of the everyday items which spoke of occupation, a discarded newspaper, a sweater lying on the settee, keys or a wallet on a side table. Sally glanced around as Brad's hands ran over the neat stack of books and papers on the table in front of him. His fingers recognised his quarry, and he turned his head, seeking Sally.

'I'm here,' she answered to give direction to his voice.

'Could you look up Harrison, Peter, and dial the number for me, please?'

More than anything, his stilted tones betrayed to Sally how this man hated to rely on anyone. He was obviously used to being in charge, and to have to ask for aid, especially from a stranger, only emphasised his present helplessness. She dialled the number of the specialist. She couldn't help noticing it was a Harley Street address, then she handed the receiver to Bradney Picton.

'It's ringing now. I'll put the kettle on, shall I?' She didn't wait for his nod of agreement but found her way to the neat kitchen whose windows gave a view of the big entrance gates to the estate. She smiled. Obviously whoever designed this lodge knew the woman of the house would spend many hours here, well placed to see if the gates needed to be opened. Then her husband would go out and vet the arrivals to guard the privacy of his masters.

In spite of rattling the kettle and the china mugs, she found hanging on hooks from a shelf of the big Welsh dresser, Sally couldn't shut out the sound of Bradney Picton's anxious voice.

'Peter? Hi! It's Brad Picton. I can't see. One minute I was trying to read the headlines of the paper and the next wham. It was as sudden as someone turning out the light. What's going on? . . . No! I'm down here at the lodge, convalescing as I promised . . . well, I did some work last night . . . I may have gone on longer than I realised . . . No! Of course not. I'm not an idiot. . . well, alright, perhaps I am an idiot, but you don't understand . . . alright, alright. Don't keep on. What can you do? How long before I can see? . . . OK. I'll get the car and be with you by two o'clock. Alright. See you then. Thanks. Goodbye.'

Sally carried the tray with two mugs of coffee, and a plate of biscuits she had found, through to the main living room of the lodge. 'Everything alright?' she enquired brightly.

Bradney Picton was feeling the touch pad of the telephone, obviously trying to punch out a number. He gave up in disgust and pushed the instrument across the table.

'Here. Can you do the honours again . . . please?' He dictated a London number as Sally dialled for him, then passed him the receiver.

'Farthing? Send Jim with the car right away. I need to see Harrison this afternoon at two o'clock. What? No, nothing's wrong. Don't fuss.'

Sally had been listening to this exchange with raised eyebrows. Who was on the other end of this conversation? How could he be so rude? As she watched, to her amazement a tide of dark red surged over Bradney Picton's face leaving a bright blush on his cheeks. His head dropped, almost in the manner of a schoolboy caught out in wrongdoing. His voice took on an apologetic tone, almost wheedling as he explained again how he had come to lose his sight.

'Oh, come on, Farthing, don't give me a hard time. Yes, I know . . . but . . . but . . . but I'm not. I have a Guardian Angel at my side right now.'

His head lifted to where he thought Sally was standing. 'Farthing wants to talk to you.'

Filled with curiosity Sally reached out and took the receiver from his hand. Who on earth had the power to reduce this authoritative man to the level of an apologetic boy?

'Hello. I'm Sally Fletcher.'

'Well, Sally Fletcher perhaps you'll tell me what's going on?'

The woman's voice was pleasant but firm, obviously used to getting the answers she wanted. She sounded as if she might have been Bradney Picton's old Nanny? Sally explained the situation as she knew it and promised to wait at the lodge until the chauffeur-driven car arrived.

'Well Bradney, it looks as though you're stuck with me for a while longer,' she smiled.

'Brad. My friend's call me Brad, and you've turned out to be a friend in need. But what about the children?'

'They get their lunch at school and my Dad'll grab a sandwich if he comes in. I cook him a proper meal in the evenings.'

'You and the children live with your father, do you?'

'Yes. I was born in that house. Dad's a joiner and cabinetmaker. He used to work for the estate when Mrs Masterson was alive. Before she died, she gave all the estate workers the opportunity to buy their own homes. It took most of Dad's savings, but he jumped at the chance. Mum always used to fret at the lack of security involved living in a tied house.'

'So now she'll be happy at any rate,' said Brad.

'My mother died when I was twelve.' Sally's voice was quiet but matter of fact. In the intervening fifteen years she had grown closer to her father and learned to manage without a mother's presence.

But Brad looked appalled at his tactlessness. Perhaps he felt life without his own mother would have been unthinkable? 'I'm sorry. I'm so sorry. You poor child.'

Sally's eyebrows were having plenty of exercise this morning. Brad had sounded, not only conventionally sorry for her loss but horrified at the thought. And where did he get off calling her a child? He couldn't be more than thirty or so himself surely?

19

'My Dad is a wonderful man. He did everything to make up for me losing Mum. I couldn't have wished for a happier and more well-balanced childhood.'

Brad opened his mouth, hesitated and then shut it once more.

Sally wondered what he had been going to say. 'How long will it be before your car comes? Will you be away overnight? Should I pack a bag for you?'

'No, thanks. If I need anything, I can get it sent over from my London flat.'

So Mr Angry was not only used to command, he also obviously had plenty of money.

'What brought you down to Little Mithering? I heard you say you were here to convalesce. But we're so out of the way, I'm surprised you've ever heard of us.'

Brad hesitated, then answered slowly. 'I first heard of the village when I saw an advertisement for the sale of the Estate. Later, when I wanted somewhere to lose myself for a while, it seemed ideal. I'd been cooped up in that hospital for so long I felt I'd go mad if I couldn't be on my own for a while.'

'What happened?'

Again Brad hesitated, then chose his words carefully. 'I was on a rig. There'd been some trouble and I went to investigate. A block slipped, swung down and hit me on the head. It threw me sideways and the other side of my head made contact with a metal stanchion. Of course I had my hard hat on. That took the main force of the blows or I wouldn't be here to tell the tale. But apparently my head got such a shaking my brain was bruised. When I left the hospital all I needed was a longish period of rest and quiet. Farthing arranged the details and I moved in three weeks ago when they finally let me go.'

'Three weeks? Good heavens, I must be slipping. How come I hadn't met you until yesterday?' She blushed again remembering their first encounter and was glad he couldn't see the evidence of her discomfort.

'I barely went out for the first ten days. Then I set myself a target of walking a little farther each day. Yesterday was my longest trip out so far.'

'And look how it ended. I really am sorry you know.'

Brad grinned. 'Yes. I know you are, but it was a very good hit, and if I hadn't met you then, who would have come to my rescue this morning? Sally? Sally? Are you still there?'

Sally's attention had wandered. Had he somehow sensed that? When Brad had smiled at her, or where he thought she was, his whole face had changed, relaxing the deep grooves which ran from his nostrils to the corners of his mouth and curving up the lips of that mouth in a most agreeable fashion. She was just wondering idly how he had come to look so severe when Brad's call brought her back to reality.

'What? Oh, yes. It was a good hit.'

Brad shook his head, obviously aware he'd lost her attention somehow but unable to account for it. 'Tell me about yourself,' he invited.

Eager to make up for her inattention and sure he needed some distraction from worrying about his eyes, Sally amused him for the next hour with tales of village life.

She said nothing of her own success as an accountant with a prestigious firm in Libchester, the big town about thirty miles away towards London.

She didn't mention her engagement to Laurence, which had ended so disastrously, nor did she touch on the wrench it had been to give up her independence and return

21

to the village when Dad needed her so much to look after the children. Some things you don't talk about to strangers and some things are no one else's business.

Chapter Three

On the long drive up to London Brad tried not to think about his own foolish actions. Peter Harrison had warned him to keep calm, get plenty of rest and most of all not to overtax his eyes. Working for hours at his laptop by artificial light had surely been the stupidest thing he could have chosen to do.

The big car purred on its way with Jim, Brad's driver, at the wheel. Jim knew exactly where to go and had driven Brad often enough to be aware his boss was not in the habit of making small talk. There was nothing to distract Brad's fearful thoughts of a future without his sight.

In desperation he tried to think of something outside his own life. The only subject not a part of his past was Sally. He smiled as he remembered her spirited defence of the children in her care. Mum would have liked Sally. They shared the same passionate love for their children. He'd bet Sally would do anything to protect those kinds from harm, just like Mum.

But who had been there to protect Sally? She said her Dad was a good man and they were close, but obviously not close enough to stop her getting pregnant . . . twice. He'd almost blurted out as much when Sally was talking of her father. But then of course there had been a fiancée. Had he been able to cope with one child, but the second proved too much?

Brad's hands clenched at the thought of Sally being abandoned and heartbroken. Poor kid. The guy must be a real slimeball to leave a young girl like that. At least she had her father. He must have taken her in when the rat deserted her. And the villagers seemed quite kindly towards her. Funny she should say Brad might ruin her reputation? What kind of reputation did a girl have left with two illegitimate children?

But from her chat before Jim arrived, she was plainly in the swing of things in the village. She ran the Brownies, played in the Tennis Club, helped with the Village Fete, belonged to the Drama Club which put on the annual pantomime and was Secretary to the Parish Council. Quite an impressive list for someone who, in another society, might find herself an outcast. Brad thought with bitterness of the slights and snubs his mother had endured in spite of her wedding ring.

Do the children have problems? Do they have to put up with teasing, bullying even? Should he be their Jock Masterson? Brad smiled, remembering the pugnacious twelve-year old boy who had raised his chin in defiance at the giant of a man who loomed over him.

'It's alright, mister. I ain't done nothing wrong.'

Outwardly cocky, while inwardly quaking, the young Brad had stood his ground.

'No-one said you did, son,' the big man had replied. 'You interested in cars then?'

Young Brad had cast a covetous eye at the sleek bodywork of the Bentley he had been polishing with his sleeve.

'I'm gonna get my Mum a car like that one day. But for meself, I'll get a Ferrari.'

The big man had laughed and applauded his choice. Then he'd gone on to discover the history of this skinny lad who, his manager had told him, hung around the garage at all hours lending a hand whenever he was allowed.

The upshot had been the enrolment of young Brad at the nearest Technical College to learn engineering and a job at the garage helping out in all his spare time. To Brad this was heaven. He was learning all about real engines and could even give Mum money he had earned. He asked nothing more of his young life.

All very well to plan things for her children thought grown-up Brad but perhaps, when Sally learned why he was really at Little Mithering, she wouldn't want to speak to him. Why hadn't he said anything when she asked why he was there? She'd given him a perfect opening when she spoke of her father buying their house. He frowned in irritation as he thought of the houses in the village which were not a part of the deal when he'd bought the estate. He'd told the truth when he said he'd heard of it through the advertisement, but he hadn't said he was the new owner. Nor had he revealed any of his plans which could drastically change the life of the village for ever. Somehow he didn't want to have to tell Sally about that until he was forced to. If she didn't like change, he didn't want to see disappointment, dislike even in her eyes. Perhaps before then he could get to know her better, be able to make her understand how his plans would benefit the local people in the long run. Everything was clear in his head. He'd written down the stages of the project, even got an artist's impression and a model made. The finance was in place and his determination to see the whole thing through. But for that he needed time, his team to be free to work on it, and most of all his own health and sight. And they might not all be in place for quite a while.

Meanwhile, Sally was telling the story she and Brad had agreed upon as she completed her abandoned shopping. She fended off Mrs Wilson's questions with seemingly candid replies.

'Yes, poor man. He was suddenly hit by a really bad migraine, possibly as a result of standing in the sun reading his paper. It is quite hot out there already you know. I just helped him back to the lodge.'

'Did you make him lie down in a dark room then, Sally love?' Mrs Wilson's tone was coy, her eyes were wide with curiosity. 'You were a long time coming back.'

Inwardly Sally cursed the road system which enabled Mrs Wilson to monitor the comings and goings of everyone in the village.

'No, no. I just made him a cup of coffee.'

'Not coffee, dear. Never coffee for a migraine,' put in Miss Jenks who was, as she put it herself, a martyr to the migraine, always had been.

'It didn't matter Miss Jenks,' said Sally. 'He didn't drink it anyway. I rang his doctor for him, and I think he's gone for an appointment this afternoon. Just the flour now Mrs Wilson, please.'

'Well that was lucky, wasn't it? Getting an appointment just like that.' Hazel Black's tone was envious. 'I suppose that classifies as an emergency, but I've had to wait a week before now for a regular appointment.'

There were nods and murmurs of agreement.

'There isn't a surgery here this afternoon,' another voice put in. 'It's the Mother and Toddler Group.'

Sally was getting desperate to leave the shop, but Mrs Wilson still held the bag of flour in her hand.

'I think it wasn't a local doctor. After all Mr Picton's only a visitor, isn't he? I expect he preferred his own man.' She reached forward and rescued the flour. 'That's all then, thank you, Mrs Wilson. I must get on. Playing the Good Samaritan has put me all behind. I'll be in for my order on Friday and settle up then. 'Bye, everyone.'

Thankfully she thrust her arm through the handle of her basket and almost used it as a battering ram to make her way through the interested group behind her. Once on the pavement she set off briskly for home, but her thoughts were with Brad, enclosed in the big car and the prison of his blindness.

Her heart had gone out to him in his frustration with the telephone keypad. Such a simple thing, to dial a number - something we take for granted every day. But without our sight even that becomes a difficult task. Sally longed to help him. He so patently hated being dependent on anyone, but what if his sight didn't return? No. She wouldn't even think that. This was just a temporary thing. Would he come straight back from his visit to the specialist? But he mentioned a flat in London. Perhaps it would be better for him to stay nearer Harley Street than return to the village?

Sally's heart sank. Perhaps Brad Picton would never come back. Why did that bother her? The thought of life without her handsome Mr Angry gave her an empty feeling. Which was ridiculous. She'd only just met the man. He couldn't mean anything to her. But, strangely, he did.

For the next two days Sally visited the lodge to see if Brad had returned. There was no answer to her knock. The doors and windows were closed tightly and when she peered through the glass, she could see no sign of occupation. On Friday she couldn't avoid going into the village shop to pick up her weekly order. She dreaded the probing questions she knew would greet her, but Mrs Wilson was giving information this morning, not seeking it.

'So our Mr Picton is going to be away for a while then Sally?'

'Really?'

'Yes. He's cancelled his papers, or rather someone did it for him. A secretary I expect.'

Sally wondered if it had been the woman Brad called Farthing.

'But it's only temporary. He'll let me know when he's coming back.'

The sun came out for Sally. She could have kissed Mrs Wilson.

'Did he . . . I mean, whoever called, say how he was feeling?'

'No. Very quiet and business-like she was, but pleasant you know. Now then Sally, anything else? You're looking very chipper today, dear. Any special reason?'

'No, Mrs Wilson. It's just such a lovely day . . . and there's the Fete tomorrow to look forward to isn't there?' Sally had to find some reason to offer for the broad smile she could feel on her face.

MrsWilson sniffed. 'Well, if you say so. It's a lot of hard work for folks but I'll say this Sally, you were never afraid to muck in and get your hands dirty. I expect I'll see you there. You have got a proper rota for the Brownies Bran Tub, haven't you? I don't want my Tiffany to be on duty all afternoon. She's entering the Little Mithering Harvest Princess competition, you know.'

Sally hid a smile. 'Yes, of course I know Mrs Wilson. She enters every year, doesn't she? There'll be a proper rota, I promise, and the children will help too. Now, I must get going and bake my entries for the cake competition and my offerings for the Refreshment Tent. Bye.'

She almost danced down the street. Brad was coming back. The man with Sean Bean's broad shoulders and long, long legs. She blushed and laughed at herself for being so excited. He hardly knew she was alive. He'd called her a child and clearly had no interest in her as a woman. But then she hadn't been seen in her best light, an impish voice in her head insisted. She thought of him so often. Was he really as good-looking as she remembered? When she recalled the deep honey-tones of his voice as they had chatted together, she caught her breath and felt a distinct weakness about the knees. This was the first time since Laurence went to the States that she had felt any interest in a man. Thank goodness she did. It might convince Dad she was well and truly over Laurence although, of course, she couldn't say anything to Dad about Bradney Picton could she? Not yet.

But he was coming back. In spite of herself she smiled again. She would find out if her memory was playing tricks or if he really was as gorgeous as he had seemed.

Chapter Four

On Monday morning a huge bouquet was delivered to the cottage for Sally. When Bob Fletcher came home for lunch he found his house contained more flowers than the garden outside. Every vase was full. Sally had even pressed into service empty jam jars destined for the recycling bin.

In answer to his look of enquiry Sally showed him the card which had arrived with the flowers.

'With grateful thanks. News is good. See you soon. Brad'.

Bob smiled.

'Quite right, pet. At least it shows the chap has some manners. And it's no more than you deserve. You're a good girl, Sally.'

He patted her shoulder briefly and sat down at the table to tackle the plate of cold meat, salad and pickles which she had laid out ready for him. Sally swallowed a lump in her throat and turned to the kitchen sink, busying herself while she gazed out of the kitchen window. Dad never said much, but she knew he appreciated the sacrifice she had made in coming home to look after the children.

When she'd gone to work in Libchester, Sally had worried about Dad being lonely without her. At first she'd returned each weekend, but when she'd left the digs and moved into her own flat she had more than enough to occupy her time. There were invitations to accept, favourite hobbies to pursue, and her own home brought domestic chores, cleaning, shopping and preparations for the week ahead at work. Life had become very full, and her visits home grew scarce. And then Laurence Pritchard had come along, the man who had eventually monopolised all her free time.

When Bob Fletcher had apprehensively told his daughter he was courting, she had been delighted. It was true that when she first met Sharon, Sally had been surprised. Dad hadn't told her of the age gap. Sharon couldn't be more than five or six years older than Sally. But she'd seemed genuinely fond of Bob Fletcher who, at fifty, was a slim, quiet, self-assured man who didn't look his age. He had a warm, slow smile and a good word for everyone. He always said having Sally and her host of friends around had kept him young. Sally had wished the happy couple joy with all her heart and had been delighted to be one of Sharon's bridesmaids.

The arrival of baby Philip had completed the little family at the cottage. Sally doted on her new half-brother and all had seemed to be going well.

However not long after Lucy was born, when Sally made her rare visits home, she had noticed a change in Sharon. The precious hours Sally spent in the village seemed to be filled with the young mother's moans of how difficult it was to manage the baby and a toddler; how demanding Philip had become since the new baby's arrival; how little sleep she got when the baby was teething; how boring it was in the village. Before her marriage, Sharon had lived in Libchester, been used to a take-away on the corner of the street and a cinema which showed three new films in a week.

As a newly-wed she had been enchanted with the picture-postcard beauty of the village and thanks to Bob Fletcher's popularity she had been warmly received by everyone. But her moans, complaints and unkind comments about other people were isolating her from the close-knit community. Bitterly she had compared her own life of drudgery to Sally's freedom, fun and financial independence.

In retrospect, it was unfortunate that Sally's life had been so full she could spare little time to soothe Sharon's envy. The younger girl hadn't really worried about the situation, believing that, as the baby grew older, things would improve. That seemed to be the pattern with her own married friends who had young families. And Dad had been through it all before. Sally had been sure he would help Sharon to cope, and everything would be alright.

In Libchester, Sally had become more and more involved with Laurence. He was fun and full of confidence. Full of self-confidence and ambition, he had plans for the future. He swept Sally along with his enthusiasm. Her job had been satisfying, her future secure. She bloomed with good health and with Laurence life had always been exciting. She'd never known what he would be planning next.

'Are you not eating, pet?'

Her father's voice pulled Sally back from bitter-sweet memories. She put a smile on her face and turned to the table.

'I only need a sandwich, Dad. I had a sinfully huge piece of Mavis Enderby's cream sponge when I was at the Vicarage for my coffee earlier.'

Bob Fletcher smiled. Mavis Enderby's delicious sponge cakes were famous far and wide.

'Right. I see what you mean. Well, I must be off. It's a grand drying day. Your washing'll be fit for the iron tonight. See you later, pet. Bye.'

With domestic chores calling her, Sally's thoughts were fixed firmly on the present for the rest of the day. She had no time to dwell on past unhappiness or her good-looking new acquaintance.

Wednesday brought a letter. Sally looked at the outside of the envelope with a little smile on her face. She felt sure it was from Bradney Picton. The writing looked like the entries she had seen in his address book when she looked up Peter Harrison's telephone number. It was firm, decisive and beautifully formed, handsome in fact. Just like the writer. Had he done his own detective work to find her address, or was that one of Farthing's duties?

She laughed, slit open the envelope and withdrew the single sheet it contained.

'Dear Sally, I'm hoping to be home Friday evening. Could you please ask Mrs Wilson to order my papers from Saturday morning – she knows which ones. I hope you and the children are well and look forward to seeing you soon. Brad.'

Short and to the point. Businesslike. Sally smiled. It would be good to see him again. She slipped the letter into her pocket. It would be worth fielding all the suggestive remarks Mrs Wilson would no doubt slide into the conversation because Sally had been the one to hear from Mr Picton. He hadn't communicated his needs directly to Mrs Wilson and her feathers would certainly be ruffled. Too bad. Roll on Saturday.

Brad cleared away his breakfast things and looked through the kitchen windows towards the big gates for the tenth time that morning. Then he laughed at himself. What a fool he was, so eager to see Sally walk up his path. But wasn't it natural? After all, the young girl had been very helpful. He wanted to thank her again. She was a really nice kid. He couldn't remember ever having been so taken with a youngster before. Perhaps it was her situation which commanded his sympathy? If only there'd been someone to help out his mother in her time of need. He hoped he could do something for Sally and the children. She must find it hard, although she was obviously a very competent young person. He closed his eyes and remembered the soothing authority in her voice. He thought how well she had taken charge of a difficult situation, guiding him home, and then being sensible about helping and sensitive to his fears while he waited for Jim to arrive with the car. He supposed the burden of parenthood had made her grow up too fast.

When the doorbell rang, Brad glanced through the kitchen window and saw a car standing outside the gates. Drat it. While he'd been daydreaming, someone had got out and come to the front door unseen. Brad muttered crossly. He didn't want any visitors - or at least only one. Could he pretend he was out and just not answer? The bell rang again and someone wielded the doorknocker to good effect. Evidently whoever was calling was not to be put off. Who on earth could it be? He put on the dark glasses Peter Harrison insisted he wore outside during the day and went to open the front door.

He was in time to see the back view of a woman who had evidently given up on him. The sun shone on glossy warm brown hair which swung to her shoulders. The pretty cotton dress she wore, belted at the trim waist, set off the curves of a delightful figure. Her long legs beneath the dress were bare and lightly tanned and on her small feet she wore dainty sandals with a low heel. Brad appreciated the picture she made.

'Hello,' he called.

She swung round, giving Brad further proof of her womanly shape. With her back to the sun her face was in shadow and Brad's dark glasses gave him little idea of her features, but his interest had been aroused.

'Can I help you?' he offered.

'Brad! You are home. How lovely. Welcome back.'

Brad frowned. That voice. As the woman came nearer her face became clear. She was gorgeous. Clear skin, given a glow by the sun; a dusting of freckles over her nose; hazel eyes which smiled warmly below beautifully arched brows and a wide, generous mouth whose full lower lip seemed familiar. His mouth dropped open.

'Brad?' she asked. 'Brad? Are you alright? You can see now, can't you?' The anxiety in her voice shook Brad out of his stupor.

'What? Who? I . . .'

'Brad. It's me. Sally.'

At last Brad was convinced it was Sally speaking. But a beautiful, grown-up, womanly Sally. He'd thought she would become a real smasher and he'd been right. But not in one week, surely?

'Hello, Sally.' He could barely get the words out. Surprise rendered him stupid.

'Can I come in?'

He stepped back to let her pass him and caught a drift of the fragrance she wore. It was like her, fresh and light. Closing the door behind her, he walked into the main living room of the lodge and took off his dark glasses. Sally laid her bag on the table and turned to face him. Without his dark glasses her face was even more appealing.

'I don't understand. You . . . you can't be . . . you've changed,' he accused her.

He saw her eyes light up with laughter. There was an imp of mischief in her voice as she chided him.

'Oh, Brad. Did you really expect me to turn up this morning in outgrown shorts and scruffy trainers?'

He grinned. 'I suppose I did. I've been picturing you all week just like that.'

'But why?' Sally frowned in bewilderment, then opened her eyes wide as she realised what had happened. 'Of course! You really only saw me in Home Park, didn't you? I forgot that all the while we walked along the road and spent time together waiting for Jim to arrive, I could see you, but you couldn't see me. The only impression you had of me was with my hair up in bunches as I played cricket with the children.' Her expression was rueful.

'It was a very nice impression,' he hastened to assure her. 'But today . . .'

'Today?' she prompted head cocked to one side awaiting his answer.

'Today's impression is much better,' he said, with a look so warmly appreciative it brought a blush to Sally's cheeks.

'I'm glad you see an improvement,' she laughed.

Chapter Five

The following days and weeks were a happy time for Sally. She loved Dad and the children dearly, but she'd been missing the kind of adult conversation she had enjoyed with her friends and colleagues at work. Since returning home there'd been no-one to share discussion of world events, especially what went on in the financial sector. Brad seemed to be exactly on her wavelength. And there was the added dimension of mutual attraction. Although never acknowledged, there was a tingle of awareness between them. Its constant presence heightened their enjoyment. Colours were brighter, jokes more amusing, ideas more inspired. They discussed everything under the sun while they drank coffee in the garden of the lodge or, later, shared gentle walks on shady days. Brad was being very good and careful not to retard his recovery this time, but without Sally's visits to distract him he would have been tempted back to his laptop.

From his breadth of knowledge, he gave Sally an insight into certain big business moves she had not understood before. She wasn't afraid to disagree vehemently with Brad's opinion if she thought she was right – a fact which amused and intrigued him.

The Sally he was getting to know certainly didn't fit the picture he had formed of a young, defenceless and helpless girl, let down by a callous, selfish boyfriend and without resources to make a life for herself. This more sophisticated, well-educated and well-informed Sally, who contradicted his pronouncements with a twinkle in her eye and teased him out of his more serious moods, was a total enigma. She fascinated him and he looked forward each morning to her arrival. Most days through the week she would make time to visit him, except Thursdays. He knew he would never see her on a Thursday.

When Sally had first come home there hadn't been enough time in the day to get everything done in the house and also spend hours trying to comfort the children and make them feel loved and secure.

She had hardly believed her father when he had telephoned her to say Sharon had gone. Gone? Gone where? Why? For how long? But Bob Fletcher hadn't been able to give her any answers.

Sharon had been a bit depressed, a bit snappy for a while, but then she'd seemed to get over that. She'd smartened herself up, had her hair re-styled and taken a pride in her appearance, almost like she used to be before the children were born. Bob had been delighted, relieved things were back to normal, and Sharon was happy again.

But it seemed her happiness hadn't come from her home and family but from the company and flattery of a certain stationery salesman. One morning in the village she'd bumped into the 'rep' who supplied Mrs Wilson. There'd been a mutual attraction and Sharon had found a way of escape from the domestic life she had come to hate.

Gradually Sally had got the hang of running a house and a family. Her father had demanded little and been pathetically grateful for all she did. The children had relaxed as time passed and Sally made no move to leave them. Eventually Lucy had stopped talking about Sharon, but Philip remembered his pretty Mummy and sometimes asked wistfully if she would ever come back. It had taken Sally a long time to convince Philip that Mummy hadn't gone away because he'd been a naughty boy.

Once she had got herself into a manageable routine with the house Sally'd thought seriously of her future. Obviously she couldn't leave Dad and the children until the kids had left school. So she must rebuild some kind of satisfactory life here in the village.

She was an excellent accountant. The firm had been very sorry to lose her. She knew they would give a glowing recommendation to anyone who wanted to vet her qualifications. It seemed the ideal plan would be to try and get a few clients she could service from home. She intended to start working part-time while the children were so young. Later, hopefully, they wouldn't rely on her so much and she could expand her client list.

As she contemplated her life over the next few years, Sally ruthlessly locked away her dreams of love and romance. The children needed her. She'd made her choice so she wouldn't whine about it. Work was the answer, lots of hard work which would leave her no time for regrets.

With Sally, to decide was to act. She had put out feelers locally and now had two clients. Twice a month, on Thursdays, she spent the morning at Major Lawson's riding stables doing his books, and in the afternoons, she could be found in the back room of the pub doing the same service for Fred Tucker. Not exactly what she had planned for her career, but it brought in some money of her own and she was using the skills of her training. Both men were so delighted with her work they offered her more clients among their friends than she could have coped with. But she was adamant. She would start small and see how her work fitted in with the family.

On her free Thursdays Sally now blitzed the cottage from top to bottom to give her more time to spend with Brad without letting her standards slip at home. She smiled as she told her father why he found his lunch plated up in the fridge more often these days.

'Bring the lad over for Sunday lunch,' was his suggestion. 'I'd like to meet him. You obviously get on well if the sparkle in your eyes these days can be relied on.'

Sally laughed.

'Don't you go matchmaking, Dad,' she warned. 'I do enjoy Brad's company. He's so easy to talk to. I didn't realise how stifled I'd been feeling, just concentrating on village life, hatches, matches and dispatches and who's turn it is to do the church flowers.' She caught her bottom lip between her teeth and looked stricken at the expression on her father's face. 'Oh, Dad. I'm sorry. I didn't mean that how it sounded.'

Bob Fletcher sighed and shook his head.

'Yes, you did, pet. Be honest now. I know it must be dull for you here after the kind of life you had in Libchester. I hate to see you so confined. Perhaps if I hired a housekeeper?'

Sally wouldn't let him finish.

'No way, Dad. How could you even suggest it? The children have had enough upset as it is. Bringing in a stranger now would undo all the good work I hope I've done over the last eighteen months.'

'You're right, of course. It would. But it's not fair that your life should be so disrupted.'

Sally walked across to the chair where he sat with a worried frown on his face, put her hand on his shoulder and bent to kiss the top of his head.

'Don't fret about it, Dad. It's alright, really. Perhaps in the new school year I'll take on another couple of clients. In the dark evenings the children will be staying in after tea and you'll be here for them. Yes. I think I will. I'd enjoy that.'

'In the meantime, get your friend Brad over. I'd like to meet him.'

Brad duly came for Sunday lunch. An amused Sally watched the two men sound each other out. It made her think of two strange dogs meeting, circling with hackles slightly raised, wary, sniffing at each other to establish a new relationship. Each seemed pleased with whatever he found in the other and the two soon settled into a pleasant friendship.

But it was Brad's relationship with the children which surprised Sally.

'Why do you always wear sunglasses, even when the sun's not shining,' Lucy wanted to know.

'Because I had an accident, and my eyes must rest. I'm not allowed to let bright lights shine in them, or read too much, 'specially in the evening when the electric light is on.'

'Can you watch the telly?'

'No.'

'Gosh! Poor Brad.' Lucy would be heartbroken if she was deprived of her favourite Telly Tubbies.

'Can you use a computer?' Philip's interest was aroused.

'I can. But I'm not allowed to at the moment.'

'That's rotten. What happened to your eyes?'

'That's enough, children,' Sally protested. 'It's not good manners to pester guests with questions.' She had been pleased, if slightly surprised, at Brad's patience with the children's curiosity.

'But he doesn't mind. Do you Brad?' Philip was quite confident this big man would tell him what he wanted to know.

Sally couldn't understand Philip's attitude. Usually he waited quite a while before becoming so assured with someone new. But Philip and Brad had hit it off immediately. She couldn't know that, in Philip, Brad saw his own young self, hiding the hurt of his abandonment and trying to be a man. Perhaps some shared emotion formed an invisible bond between them?

Sunday lunch at the cottage became a regular ritual.

A week after the beginning of the Summer holidays, Peter Harrison gave Brad the go-ahead to take off his glasses.

Lucy was delighted. On The following Sunday after lunch she climbed up onto Brad's lap where he sat at ease in one of the big armchairs near the kitchen range. Having settled herself comfortably she took his face in her small hands and turned it towards her own.

'I'm glad you haven't got those horrid glasses anymore,' she confided. 'Now I can see you.'

'But you've been seeing Brad for ages, silly,' scoffed Philip.

The adult's eyes met over the two children's heads.

'Out of the mouths of babes,' quoted Bob.

'The eyes are the windows of the soul,' quoted Brad back at him with a grin. 'I'm glad I haven't got them on too, Lucy. I couldn't see properly what a pretty little girl you are,' he added tickling her ribs which produced squeals of delight.

Sally watched Brad's interaction with the children with pleasure. It was good for them. She was the sole relative they had besides their parents. Bob and Sharon had both been only children. Sharon's parents lived abroad and after she had left, they had shown no interest in keeping in touch with their grandchildren. Philip and Lucy had adopted Brad as a sort of honorary uncle, and he played the part well. Where had he learned the trick of treating children as equals, she wondered? He had told her he had no brothers or sisters therefore it hadn't been with nephews or nieces. Godchildren perhaps? He'd make a wonderful father. At this point Sally checked her thoughts and declared it was far too nice a day to stay indoors. What should they do?

'Cricket.' voted Philip.

Sally wasn't sure. She looked questioningly at Brad.

'It's alright. I think a gentle game wouldn't hurt me. As long as you promise not to give it as good a hit as last time I saw you play,' he teased Philip.

By this time Philip was so at ease with Brad, he just laughed.

'You'll have to learn to duck,' he chuckled and ran off to get the cricket things.

As they strolled through the trees following the children Brad gently approached the subject of the children's absent father. He couldn't help wondering if Sally still nursed a broken heart. She seemed happy enough and self-contained, but did she feel anger and betrayal?

'Did the children's father teach Philip to play cricket. He seems to have been an apt pupil.'

Sally laughed. 'Heavens no. Dad made the stumps and bails and gave Philip his bat, but I taught him the rudiments. I used to play years ago at school, but I don't remember all the terms and technicalities.'

'Not so many years ago, surely?'

Sally stopped and turned to Brad with a smile. 'Just how old do you think I am, Brad? When we first met you called me a child and from odd things you said then you thought me much younger than I am. While I suppose that could be thought flattering in a way, you surely don't still think I'm a little girl?'

Brad looked down at her. His eyes travelled in appreciation over her shapely body and came back to rest on her face. She smiled up at him with such open honesty, he caught his breath. When had he last had such an uncomplicated relationship with anyone? She asked nothing of him but his friendship. All his life it seemed, certainly since he was seven years old, people had relied on him, for money, jobs, answers, directions and decisions, both difficult and unpleasant. Even Farthing, who knew more about him than anyone now living, still looked to him for her livelihood and instructions on future actions. Sally had slipped into his life so gently he couldn't put a finger on when she had become so essential to his everyday content. She asked nothing of him, made no demands.

That's because she doesn't know who you are, said a mean voice in his head. It wouldn't make any difference, he answered himself. But was he sure? If Sally knew who he really was and why he was here, would she turn away from him in anger and disgust, or would the acquisitive light appear in her eyes as she realised what a good catch he would be? He'd seen it many times before. Hey! When did marriage come onto the agenda?

'Well?' demanded Sally. 'Have you decided yet? Or are you so afraid of hurting my feelings you daren't say how ancient you have discovered me to be?'

Brad shook his head. He'd been staring at Sally without seeing her as his thoughts went round and round.

Now he looked again, properly. Her upturned face was open to the closest inspection. He thought it was perfect – except perhaps for the small worry frown between her delicately shaped eyebrows. That had no doubt been caused by the results of her fiancée's defection. Brad's lips tightened in anger. How could anyone leave such a beautiful, warm-hearted girl as Sally. Now the frown deepened as she saw the expression his face. Quickly he assumed a thoughtful look.

'Considering Philip is now seven, I suppose you must be at least twenty-three?' he offered.

Sally laughed and shook her head. 'No, you're way out. I was twenty when Philip was born. Although what that's got to do with anything I don't know.'

'Nothing, of course. Nothing at all,' Brad hastened to assure her. Heavens. He didn't want her to think he was judging her or drawing attention to a teenage pregnancy. But hang on. It hadn't been, had it? The mystery of Sally deepened as Brad realised how much older she had been when she became pregnant. Why hadn't they practised birth control? Mrs Wilson had spoken of a fiancée, so they were presumably going to get married. Why didn't they do it when Sally became pregnant? Or was the fiancée Mrs Wilson spoke of not the children's father? Brad was becoming more confused the more he learned about Sally.

The game of cricket was huge fun and enjoyed by all. Philip was delighted to discover what a good bowler Brad was. Sally appreciated the skill with which Brad gave seemingly difficult deliveries while making sure that Philip would be able to hit enough of them to keep up his interest and pleasure in the game.

When Philip gave one ball a particularly good smack, Sally and Brad ran from different directions to intercept it.

It became a race to see who could get there first. Sally started to laugh which impeded her progress and just as she reached her target she tripped. Her hands flew out and gripped Brad's shirtfront, just as his arms went round her to stop her falling. She looked up with sparkling eyes full of laughter which stilled as she saw his face. Suddenly she was conscious of Brad's strong arms around her, crushing her to the broad chest where his heart thudded against his ribs with a force she could feel. As she looked, his eyes grew darker. Slowly his head lowered to hers. Of themselves her lips parted to accept his kiss. She could feel his warm breath on her cheek.

'Come on, you two. I've got hundreds of runs. You are alright aren't you, Sally?'

Brad's eyes closed in frustration. When he opened them, he saw the hint of regret in hers. His smile was rueful. As he released her he drew one finger gently the length of her flushed cheek.

'Later,' he promised quietly.

But there was to be no 'later' for them that evening. After Brad had stayed to share supper with the family at the cottage, Sally was involved in seeing the children to bed. Bob Fletcher invited Brad to join him at the pub for a quiet drink to recover from a day spent with the children. Brad hesitated only a moment before accepting. He enjoyed the time spent in Bob's company but learned nothing new about Sally and the children.

'It's nice to hear the children call her Sally,' he had remarked, but Bob's answer only seemed to confirm what Brad thought he knew about the set up at the cottage.

'Yes. We thought anything else would be a bit stuffy, considering how young she was when they were born,' Sally's father had answered remembering Sharon's horror

46

at someone's suggestion that, because of the age gap, her children could call Sally, Aunty. It had made Sharon feel as old as if Sally would have called her 'stepmother'. So that suggestion had been knocked on the head.

On his walk home that evening Brad tried to sort out his thoughts and his feelings for Sally. Where was this relationship going? He certainly felt drawn to Sally. After the incident during the cricket match, he was sure there was a definite spark between them. And he was on the way to feeling for her something much deeper than he could have thought possible. But was there a future there? Should Sally be a permanent part of his life? That would mean marriage and taking on someone else's children. For him commitment was the only way forward where children were concerned. He had always avoided anything but the lightest of relationships in the past, not ready to pledge himself to any of his lady friends. He had never regretted parting from them, gently, and usually with a handsome present, to soothe their hurt pride. He was convinced he had never broken any woman's heart.

But Sally was different. She wasn't chasing him, or even dallying so that he could catch her. She didn't flirt with him or provide openings for them to be alone in a romantic situation. With two kids around that would prove difficult. Brad grinned. What a bighead he had become. Here he was wondering if he should pursue the relationship further when, despite the tug of physical attraction between them, he didn't even know if Sally had any deeper feelings for him. Perhaps she just liked him as a friend, someone she had rescued from fear and loneliness.

That thought made Brad stop dead in his tracks. He didn't like the idea Sally could simply be sorry for him.

He didn't like it at all, but it would be just like her generous nature to take pity on someone who needed her. Brad frowned. He wanted reassurance Sally's feelings for him were stronger than that. But if so, where did that leave Sally? Soon now he must confess what connection he really had with the Estate. Soon everyone would know and when his plans were passed, and the builders moved in there may well be some unhappy residents in the village. What then? Where would Sally stand? If he wasn't prepared to go the whole way with her, he should end their friendship now. But deep in his heart Brad knew he never wanted to let Sally go. She had turned him upside down, laughing at him, contradicting and teasing him, caring nothing for his wealth and status, because she was unaware of it. She had brought light and laughter to Brad's existence where for so many years there had only been the grey monotony of work and mistrust. With Sally around life was fun. He couldn't go back. He wouldn't.

Chapter Six

When her father came home from the pub and went up to bed, Sally didn't feel like sleeping. She wandered round the cottage garden in the cool aftermath of the sunny day. When she came to the sturdy swing hanging from the apple tree, which Bob had renewed since her childhood, she sat on its wooden seat and pushed off with the toe of her shoe. While she swung gently, her thoughts were on Brad. Not since Laurence had she felt such a rush of physical attraction to any man. Her body tingled as she relived those brief moments in his arms. What would have happened if the children hadn't been around? But then, they would always be around - for the next few years at least. What if? What if she and Brad, or any man, wanted to get married? What should she do? It wouldn't be so bad if he lived locally. She could still help Dad with the children and still work from home. But what if her imaginary lover lived far away, or wanted to move away? What then?

She'd made that decision once, with Laurence. How hard it had been at the time. She could still see the amazement on his face and hear the disbelief in his voice when she told him she couldn't go to America with him, at least not right away.

'You're not serious? Sally! This is the chance of a lifetime. I've got this fantastic job with Merry and Foulds. With your qualifications and past record you'll walk into a position with a salary you couldn't even dream about over here. I've already set you up with two interviews. We'll live like lords. In fact, I predict we'll soon be millionaires. Dollars perhaps, at first, but give us time. What a life we'll have. Plenty of money, a nice apartment with a good address, then a country retreat, a boat perhaps, and a decent car, one each, although in New York you don't need one. Perhaps it would be better to subscribe to a chauffeur service.'

'But Laurence, there are the children.'

'No. No children. Who needs them? They'll only complicate things. But I suppose if you really want one, we could get it a good Nanny. You wouldn't have to take much time off work. Yes, alright. We'll have one, a son to take over the fortune we're going to make, keep the name of Pritchard alive for the future.'

When Sally had been able to make him understand she was talking about her father's children, her half-brother and sister, he'd been even more incredulous.

'Don't be stupid, Sally. They're nothing to do with you. For Heaven's sake do grow out of this obsession with your family. You're a big girl now. You don't need them. You've got me.'

'But they need *me*, Laurence. How could I desert the children? Their little world has been turned upside down. I must try to reassure them they are safe. And Dad is so lost.'

'You don't owe them anything. Get a grip. We leave for New York in two weeks, together . . . or I go on my own. Your choice.'

The hint of a sad smile touched Sally's lips. Until the very last minute, Laurence had not believed she wouldn't be with him on his flight. Her rejection of him in favour of her father and a couple of brats was totally unacceptable. She had never realised he had no concept of loyalty, even loyalty to those one loved. Laurence's ego couldn't absorb her rejection. But she had made her choice and never regretted it.

There had been times when she had wondered what an exciting life in New York would have been like really, but Laurence was never a part of those imaginings. In his arrogance and rejection of values Sally held dear, he had revealed a side of himself which extinguished the love she'd felt, or thought she had felt, for him.

But Brad was different. He loved the kids and was so good with them. That didn't mean he'd want to take them on. Hey! Where did that spring from? She was getting a bit ahead of herself, wasn't she? Her relationship with Brad was so new, so tentative. They hadn't even kissed yet, so why were her thoughts running ahead so fast? Because it felt right? Because the thought of spending the rest of her life with Brad filled her with a certainty that it would be wonderful? Brad would never hurt her, like Laurence had done, never expect her to abandon her family and all her principles. How did she know that? Instinct? And if it happened that her future did lie with Brad, he wouldn't be asked to take on Philip and Lucy, would he? They were Dad's children. Surely a way could be found to sort out the problem? The hypothetical problem, she corrected herself with a grin.

What about Brad? How much longer would he be around? Once he got the all-clear from Peter Harrison he'd have to go back to work. Where? When he'd had the accident, he'd been on a rig, he said. An oil rig? She hadn't asked, wanting only that he forget the horrible results and look forward to his recovery. But if he jetted off around the world troubleshooting, presumably he had to have a base in the UK? So why not here, in Little Mithering?

Sally smiled at the path her thoughts were following. So many ifs and buts, and all running ahead of reality. She couldn't deny the attraction she felt for Brad. It grew stronger every day as he spent so much time with her and her family. She'd grown used to his presence. He fitted in so well, except for times when he seemed to hold back, as though his mind went somewhere else. Perhaps it was time to find out more about Brad.

Although Laurence had killed her love by his attitude, it had still been a very painful time at a stage in her life when she would have welcomed some support. She had given up so much, more than her father would ever know. And that's how she intended it to stay. But what if there was a way? She slipped from the swing and made her way indoors. Brad, the man of mystery. It was time to find out if Sally dared let herself love again.

The next few days followed the pattern set on Brad's return from his appointment with Peter Harrison. The children were on holiday and Sally was glad of Brad's company in entertaining them. Only a subtle change in his relationship with Sally threatened the contentment of the sunny days together. Pauses appeared in conversations which formerly had flowed so easily. Both Sally and Brad were tempted to ask questions, but too wary to voice them aloud. A new kind of tension grew which neither could break through. As the week passed, this became unbearable. On Friday morning Brad asked Sally out for dinner the next evening.

'That would be lovely, Brad. It seems ages since I went out in the evening. Time goes by so quickly I just can't believe how long it's been.'

'Shall I order a taxi? Is there any place special you'd like to go? I have no idea what's on offer in the area. Perhaps somewhere in Libchester?'

Sally thought for a moment. There were plenty of good restaurants in Libchester, but also a strong likelihood they would run into one or other of her many friends in the town. She had lost touch with some of them since her return to the village. All the more reason for friends to make a bee-line for her company and a catch-up chat. But she had the feeling this dinner date was to be a turning point in her relationship with Brad, for better or worse. She didn't want any distractions.

'I'd like to go to a pub I know down by the river, on the other side of Libchester. It's renowned for its good food, although everyone who has been there tries to keep it secret. It would be awful if it were spoiled. But it is a bit out of the way. Why don't we take my car? I don't mind driving. In fact if we could set off in good time, there's a call I need to make in town. Then, as we haven't booked already, we'd be more likely to get a table if we arrive early.'

She had a hard job to assure Brad she didn't mind driving and taking soft drinks with her meal, but once that was agreed, Sally looked forward to the next day with pleasure and mounting excitement.

The trouble she took with her appearance drew a loud wolf whistle from her young brother.

'Philip. Where on earth did you learn to do that?'

'It was on the telly, and Dick Thresher said it's what boys do when girls look nice. And you do, Sal, really pretty.'

'Pretty Sally,' agreed Lucy, stroking the skirt of Sally's deceptively simple dress. Her usual garb was practical jeans or trousers and cotton skirts or shorts for hotter weather. It was such a long time since she had worn anything so sophisticated, Sally felt like a little girl dressed up in her mother's clothes.

'Well thank you both. Here's Brad now.'

'Where are we going, Sally?' asked Lucy jumping up and down in anticipation.

Brad heard her question as he entered the room, and turned horrified eyes on Sally, making her giggle.

'We, that is Brad and I, are going out to dinner. You, my poppets, are staying here with Dad. You can help him in the garden and, if you're very good, I've left strawberries and ice cream in the fridge for you to have before bedtime.'

Ignoring their protests, she kissed each of them and swept Brad out of the cottage before his heart could be softened by Lucy's beseeching eyes.

As Sally was driving, Brad had leisure to observe her closely. She looked lovely. Any man would be proud to be seen in her company. The artful draping of her bodice clung lovingly to her full, feminine shape, while from her neat waist the well-cut skirt swung enticingly with every step she took. Her hair shone with health and vigorous brushing, its red lights adding depth and mystery to the warm brown colour. When she had greeted him with such a mischievous smile at young Lucy's remark, he had seen the lights of laughter in her eyes. With a catch of the heart he realised how much laughter and joy she had introduced into his life, how easily they communicated. He remembered how often they had been on the same wavelength on various subjects. What a wonderful companion Sally was. Could he imagine life without her? Could he bear to go back to the bleak and lonely existence where work and more work was his only constant source of pleasure and achievement? Was he to turn his back on the fun and laughter she had brought to him? The thought filled him with horror.

'Are you any good at DIY?' Sally's question interrupted his anxious thoughts.

'DIY?' Brad was jerked back to reality. 'I can swing a hammer, I suppose, but I've never had any occasion to do any domestic jobs . . . not since I was a young lad anyway,' he amended, remembering the make do and mend he and his mother had practised. 'Why do you ask?'

'I have to go and see the flat. Mr and Mrs Clark seem to have a huge list of jobs they swear are absolutely necessary and I'm not sure I have the knowledge to realise if they are right. I could get a workman in to tell me, I suppose, but it would probably be in his interest to say they all needed doing. So, if you wouldn't mind, I'd quite like you to come in with me, for moral support.' She turned her head briefly to smile at him.

Brad had no idea what she was talking about but, for that smile, he would follow her anywhere.

By this time they had reached Libchester and Sally was driving down a pleasant road of tall old houses. From the number of doorbells on the walls beside front doors it seemed most had been modified into flats.

She pulled up at a house identical to its neighbours except for the colourful window-boxes set on the broad sills, and the shine of fresh paint on the front door.

'Are you coming?' she asked Brad.

'Lead on.'

With a key from her handbag Sally opened the big front door with its stained-glass panels and made her way to the back of a wide pleasant entrance hall. Here stairs led down to a solid door on which there was a brass number 15A, a Yale lock, a bell-push and a spy-hole. She rang the bell and waited. In the silence which followed Sally looked at her watch.

'They said they were going to be home all day,' she remarked. 'I hope we haven't had a wasted journey.'

Just as she raised her hand to ring the bell again there came the sound of bolts being drawn back. The door opened enough for a head to peer around the edge.

'Who's that?' asked the head with a nod in Brad's direction.

'As you could see through the spy-hole, he's with me,' Sally answered in a pleasant but firm tone. 'Do let us in Mr Clark. We have another appointment this evening.'

The door was opened just enough for them to squeeze past the thin man who held it as if repelling boarders. His suspicious eyes took in every detail of Brad's appearance.

Sally walked through the small square entrance-hall and into a large, well-appointed sitting room. A bay window took up most of one wall and looked into the front garden across a small courtyard which had once been the basement area of the original house. Now it held large urns of plants, mangers on the walls, also sporting flowering plants, and a small fountain dripping into a shallow basin; altogether a lovely spot for an alfresco meal or a quiet evening drink.

'Now then, Mr Clark,' Sally had a list in one hand, a pen in the other. 'Shall we go through this together?'

'Where's the man from the agency?' Mr Clark's voice was an anxious whine.

'As he has no authority to make any decisions on this matter, it was hardly worth dragging him out on a Saturday evening. Shall we get on?'

Brad followed Sally and Mr Clark back into the entrance hall. From there they inspected the long narrow fitted kitchen, then along a wide passage, almost a small room, which led off the entry hall to a large airy bedroom and its adjoining dressing room. They ended up walking from the sitting room through a wide arch into a dining room with French windows giving onto a walled garden. As they went Mr Clark's whining voice kept up a constant complaint. Encouraged no doubt by Sally's lack of argument, his complaints became louder and more aggressive. Meanwhile Sally took in everything he said, looked closely at the subjects he was moaning about and made notes on her list. But when they reached the French windows she stopped short.

'No! Really, Mr Clark. That's too bad.' Her sharp exclamation of dismay startled Brad as much as Mr Clark, who was left silent with his mouth hanging open. 'The garden is an absolute disaster. You know very well that a condition of your lease is to keep the garden neat and tidy and to, at least, water the plants in dry weather. If you were going to flout these rules I can't understand why, knowing I was coming today, you didn't at least make some effort, some pretence at complying.'

Brad could see Sally was really distressed. Angry tears stood in her eyes. He looked through the French windows. Presumably there was supposed to be a lawn there. At present it looked more like a hay field in which lay one or two abandoned objects. Brad thought one of them might be an old perambulator. He couldn't even guess at the other, it was so buried in the long grass. The espaliered trees on the walls seemed in reasonable condition but the beds beneath them were choked with weeds. An overflowing dustbin stood just outside the French windows on a patio of mellow old bricks which were covered in discarded cigarette butts.

'And who has been smoking here?' Sally asked.

Brad's eyes had already spotted the nicotine stains on Mr Clark's fingers which were an answer in themselves. The man opened his mouth, but Sally was before him.

'That settles it. The flat is only for rent to non-smokers. I know there are only three months of your lease to run,' she said sternly. 'I have made a note of your complaints. Only a few of them I agree with. However I shall not be taking any action on them until after your tenancy is up. According to the lease, as you have broken the terms, I could have you evicted now, but I shall give you those three months in which to find alternative accommodation. At the end of that time, you must leave. The agent will examine the premises. The cost of any damage, breakages, or contraventions he finds will be deducted from the deposit he holds. Is that understood?'

Brad watched this girl he had got to know, he thought, so well. Her dignity was beyond doubt, so was her anger. She fixed the now shrinking Mr Clark with a cold look and waited for his reply.

'You can't do that,' he whined. 'You can't throw us out.'

'Watch me,' said Sally sternly. Her air of authority was impressive. 'And don't try to do a runner or create any further damage. I have friends who live above you, on either side and across the road. Any funny business and the police will be called immediately.'

As the door closed behind them Brad heard a string of unrepeatable curses directed at Sally's back. She said nothing but hurried to the car. Once Brad was in and belted up, she took off as if the hounds of hell were after her. She swung the car round the corner at the top of the road, turned left into the parking space beside a small park, stopped the car, switched off the engine, and burst into tears.

Quickly Brad undid his seat-belt and gathered her into his arms. 'Shush, shush,' he soothed, stroking her hair. 'It's alright. It's alright. I've got you. I'm here.' He had no idea why she was so upset but, if it was in his power, he would put it right.

'Sorry,' Sally sobbed. 'I'm being an idiot, but I couldn't bear it. My poor little flat. And then my lovely garden was the last straw.' She sobbed again. 'And I hate being nasty, especially to nasty people. It makes me feel dirty.'

Brad could feel her trembling. He pulled a snowy handkerchief from his pocket and mopped her streaming eyes, then tucked it into her hand. 'Blow.' he commanded. 'Have a good one.'

Sally gave a watery chuckle which turned into a hiccough, but she stopped crying and did as he had bidden her.

'Do you want me to go and wring that miserable little worm's neck for you,' offered Brad.

Sally shook her head. 'No. I've given him his marching orders. That's enough for him. If anybody's neck needs wringing, it's the agent's. Wait till I get hold of him. He obviously hasn't done an inspection for ages, or he would have seen the state of the place. And how he can have let it go to someone like that I don't know. He had his instructions. They were plain enough, but I suppose he thought I'd have my hands too full at home to do any inspections myself. And he was right. I should have been over before now. But my time always seems to be taken up with other things. And I suppose, if I was being honest, I didn't want to come and see anyone else in possession there.'

'It has a lot of potential.'

'Not just potential. It used to be so beautiful. I don't know when the windows or bathroom were last cleaned and did you see those nets. They were grey.'

Brad felt it safer to simply nod in agreement. If Sally said it was so, it must be.

'And the garden. We used to have parties out there. My friends live in the two flats above. It was such fun.'

Brad was in no hurry for Sally to recover enough to move on. He enjoyed the feel of her in his arms. Her head rested nicely in the hollow of his shoulder. Her light scent was in his nostrils. Her silky hair brushed his jaw. He would happily have spent the whole evening sitting there. But Sally pushed herself upright, gave a last sniff, tidied her hair with her hands and tucked his handkerchief into her bag.

'I'll wash it for you. Thank you, Brad.'

'What for? My handkerchief?'

She laughed. 'That, yes. But also for letting me cry all over you.'

'Did I have an option?' he smiled one eyebrow raised in interrogation. He had no idea of the effect that look had on Sally, or he would have used it more often.

She laughed again. 'No. Poor Brad. You didn't. Come on. Let's get going. I'm better now. I hope we can get a decent table.'

Further revelations had to wait until they had reached the pub, been shown to a secluded table and eaten a delicious meal. Their conversation throughout the evening was general and relaxed. Sally's outburst of weeping had washed away the reserve that had crept between them, but Brad felt it better to wait until they didn't have their mouths full, before broaching the questions he had in his heart. Before he started on them, something else was nagging at his mind. A topic safely removed from feelings and personal relationships.

'Why did you go to that flat today? Does the estate agent employ you to do checks or something?'

Sally looked at him with a frown. 'No, of course not. I had to go because they wanted all those things done. No-one else could authorise them so it had to be me.'

'But why? I don't understand.'

'Because I'll be paying for them, of course. It's my flat.'

Brad's face was a picture of bafflement. 'Your flat? But you live with your Dad.'

'Now, yes. But I used to live and work in Libchester. That's when I bought the flat. I was earning good money and it seemed ridiculous to waste

61

it paying rent. Besides, I like my own place. It's a lovely flat, Brad. You should see it when it's all clean and sweet-smelling. The French windows open onto the garden. I used to have breakfast in the courtyard, and we'd have dinner on the patio. On warm summer evening my friends would come and join us.'

'Us?' Brad couldn't resist asking.

'My fiancée, Laurence, and I.' Sally's smile was regretful but not tragic. 'That was in happier days. But then, when Dad needed me, I had to come back to the village. But I'll kill that agent for letting the flat to the Clarks. I pay him a whacking percentage of the rent each month and he seems to do nothing to earn it.'

Brad couldn't let her drift off the subject. He was determined to learn as much as he could about Sally this evening, and she didn't seem to be too upset by talk of the past.

'So when did you come back to the village?'

'About eighteen months ago.'

Eighteen months. That would be when Philip was nearly six and Lucy just a baby of three.

'The flat would have been pretty small for you and the children.'

'Oh, yes. But taking them to the flat was never an option. It would have been cruel to take them away from everything familiar and besides they would have missed Dad.'

'Your father's very close to them, isn't he?'

Sally's face was sad. 'Yes. They're all he's got left of Sharon. Despite everything that happened, he did love her. Perhaps he still does.'

Brad was confused.

'Sharon?'

'Their mother. She was very pretty, and young of course. I suppose I should have been more aware, more helpful, but such marriages have worked in the past. She seemed genuinely devoted to Dad.'

Her words floated past Brad's ears. His mind was whirling. This couldn't be true, could it? What about everything he'd heard and been told?

'Brad? What is it? What's the matter? You're looking very strange.'

'This Sharon. She was your father's wife and Philip and Lucy's mother? Is that right?'

'Of course. It was all very sad. She just couldn't cope and eventually ran off with a stationary salesman. Brad? What's the matter? It isn't funny you know. Why are you laughing?'

But Brad was beyond control. He had started to laugh as soon as Sally confirmed Sharon was the children's mother. He laughed and he laughed. He couldn't stop. He whooped with laughter and gasped for breath. Tears streamed down his cheeks. Diners at other tables turned to see what was so amusing but Sally sat and stared. In answer to their enquiring glances, she shrugged her shoulders. She had no idea what had got into Brad. At last he seemed to be calming.

'Brad what is it? Do you know Sharon?'

But the mention of the children's mother set Brad off again. He was helpless and he gasped and wheezed, trying to breathe and regain control. Sally passed him his own handkerchief.

'Here. You'd better have this back. Mine would be much too small for you.'

He took it and mopped his streaming eyes. This time he managed to get control and could breathe

63

properly again. He shook his head. 'Let's go outside and sit by the river. We've quite a bit of sorting out to do, my lovely Sally.'

The waiter brought them a pot of coffee to a small table by the water's edge. Brad poured Sally a cup then settled back in his chair.

'Tell me. Why has everyone let me think you were the children's mother?'

Sally, who was just taking her first sip of hot coffee, spluttered and nearly choked. 'Me? The children's mother? For goodness sake! You thought *I* was the kids mother? But why? What on earth put such a ludicrous idea into your head?'

Brad began to tick off the reasons on his fingers. 'When we first met you said you were in charge of them.'

'So I was. I am, but that doesn't mean I was their mother.'

'I agree,' said Brad. 'I thought you were the babysitter. Much too young to be their mother . . . especially in those shorts,' he added with a wicked grin.

Sally blushed but wouldn't be deflected. 'So carry on. What next?'

'The following day Mrs Wilson said what a wonderful little mother you were to the children.'

'Did she really?' Sally was touched. 'I always thought she disapproved of me and the way I try to bring them up.'

'On the contrary. It was her singing your praises that put me on the wrong track.'

'But surely, since then there must have been times when you realised the truth?'

'You'd think so, wouldn't you, but no. When I asked about the children's father teaching them cricket, you just laughed and said no. Well, of course now I know, for Bob, it's football in the winter and tennis in the summer. But when you said Dad had made the stumps for Philip I took it as a present from your Dad, Philip's grandfather, to his grandson.'

'OK. I'll give you that, but there must have been other things?'

'When Bob said you were too young to be called anything but Sally by the children, I assumed he meant the alternative was Mother, but if not, what did he mean?'

'A friend of Sharon's said I should be Aunt Sally. You can imagine how I felt about that?' Sally's voice was expressive. Brad chuckled. 'Thankfully, Sharon was horrified by the idea, so nothing came of it. Oh, Brad. What a muddle.'

Brad was thoughtful for a moment. 'Yes it was. All innocent, of course. But misunderstandings can make big problems if we let them. I should have been more thorough but saw no reason to question what I'd been told. At least tonight we've straightened things out . . . some things anyway.'

Chapter Seven

From then on there was a subtle change in Brad's attitude to Sally. He looked at her with new eyes. No longer the children's mother with a tormented past, but a free agent, a warm, attractive woman, and one who was such a major part of his present life.

Without quite knowing why the change had come about Sally noticed the difference. Always courteous, Brad was now even more attentive to her needs and wishes. He lifted burdens she was well used to carrying, amused the children so she could sit and do nothing for half an hour, and when she caught his eyes on her they held a look which made her heart flutter and her breath catch in her throat.

At least once a week he took her out to dinner. Now his eyes were on the mend, he hired a small car and when Sally wasn't free to be with him, he took to exploring the countryside to find delightful new places to entertain her. On these occasions, without the children's constant interrupting presence they learned more and more about each other.

'What about this fiancée of yours?' Brad asked one evening as they drank coffee after another delicious meal. 'Does it hurt to talk about him now?'

'No. It's all water under the bridge. That time seems so long ago and unimportant now.' She told him of Laurence, his hopes and ambitions and how her life had changed when Sharon left the village.

Brad looked at her for a long time, then reached out to cup her cheek with a gentle hand.

'You are quite some person, Sally Fletcher,' he said at last. 'I wonder if Bob truly realises all you gave up for his sake? Independence, your lovely flat and all your friends, your career and even your fiancée. It's quite a list. Do you ever miss it all? Do you ever wonder what it would have been like?'

'Of course I do. Don't make me out to be a saint, Brad. I didn't want to go back to the village and give it all up, but there was no other way. Dad and I had always been a good team, there for each other through everything. I couldn't abandon him when he was so vulnerable.

'He'd been dealt a double whammy. He'd lost his wife and couldn't cope with the children and his expanding business. He needed the work to pay for the kids so what was I to do? Swan off to the States and forget about him? I don't think so.'

'There are plenty who would have done just that, glad to get away.'

'Not if they'd been brought up by my father they wouldn't. Dad taught me values which I hold dear. That was something Laurence could never understand.'

'Yes. What about Laurence? It must have been so hard for you. Do you still miss him and that life he promised you?'

'I'd be lying if I said I never thought about what New York would have been like, the new experiences and the excitement. But funnily enough, Laurence never figures in my imaginings. Of course I was devastated when he left like that. It was a time when I really needed someone to support me. As it was, I seemed to be supporting everyone else and it was hard.'

Brad's strong warm hand reached across the table and took hers in a comforting grip. She smiled at him briefly and went on.

'The children were so lost, poor darlings, they needed lots of cuddles and reassurance. The love they gave me in return warmed my aching hear . . . and my hurt pride I suppose. Obviously Laurence thought more of his job in the States than his relationship with me. He wasn't even prepared to compromise or wait for me to join him.' She gave a rueful smile. 'But he did me a favour in the end. He just wasn't good enough for me,' she finished defiantly, with a toss of her head.

Brad laughed and let her go so he could clap his hands in agreement. Sally grinned.

'I really do believe the saying that when one door closes, another opens,' she added.

'That's what my mother used to say,' Brad murmured.

'What was she like?' Sally wanted to know.

Brad told her of his mother's hard life trying to look after herself and young Brad in a strange town and with little qualifications to earn her own living.

'She was small and gentle, almost helpless, really. I think that's probably what first attracted my father to her. Some men need their egos fed by being bigger, stronger and more capable than a woman. That works fine if they can keep it up, if they're prepared to look after her. But if they're lazy, impatient bastards who drink their pay and can't understand why the delicate young girl they married hasn't turned into a strapping, capable housewife who can also earn money for groceries, then the whole thing ends in disaster.' Brad's jaw was clenched, his nostrils pinched and his eyes were stormy as he looked back into the past.

This time it was Sally who reached for Brad's hand, to hold and stroke it in wordless sympathy.

'When he finally left us, I don't know how she coped. He'd bullied and taunted her so much, even the things she had felt capable of doing before had become a nightmare for her. I tried to help.' His lips twisted. 'I was seven years old. But I remember.'

'Poor Brad. Poor little boy. You were just Philip's age now.'

'I know. I feel a real affinity with young Philip. But he's lucky. He has his Dad and you and a whole support group at school and his mates in the village. I was always the odd one out.'

'But what on earth did you do?'

'Survived somehow. Finally, when I was twelve, Jock came along and changed my life.'

'Jock? Did your mother marry again?'

'Oh, no. Jock was married. He took me under his wing, got me trained as an engineer and gave me a job. Once I was fully trained, I became his gopher.'

'Gopher?'

Brad laughed. 'Yes. Go for this and go for that. Jock was a very successful businessman. By the time I could be useful to him he had interests all over the world. He sent me wherever he wanted to find out things. I was a sort of investigator, messenger boy, right hand man and trouble shooter, all in one.'

'He must have put a lot of trust in you?'

'He did. He knew I'd never let him down. At first it was hard. I was young and inexperienced. Older men, who'd worked for Jock longer, didn't like having to tell me what I wanted to know. I learned to keep my mouth shut and my ears open and gradually I earned respect. Jock taught me so much. Not only about business, but about life. He taught me to shoot in Canada, to fish in Australia and to play roulette in Monte Carlo. He took me in hand and showed me how to read a menu, appreciate good food and wine and how to dress. And he paid me well.'

'I'm sure you earned it.'

'I did. Jock used to say a fool and his money were soon parted. If you'd earned it the hard way, you'd appreciate it.'

'Your mother must have been so proud of you.'

A shadow crossed Brad's face. His head drooped and he didn't say any more for a long moment.

'Brad? What is it?' Sally's gentle, concerned voice reached Brad in that place to which his thoughts had retreated. He sighed and looked up into Sally's anxious eyes.

'It was almost too late, Sally,' he said quietly. 'By the time I had bought her a nice little house and seen she had nothing to worry about, it was as if she had just waited to be sure I had made it, that I was going to be alright. She was proud of me and so happy each time I came home from a trip and went to see her, but she just faded away. Why wasn't I enough for her? Why couldn't she wait with me and enjoy the good times?'

The tears were standing in Sally's eyes long before Brad put his anguished question. She bit her lip as the salty drops slid down her cheeks.

'You made her happy Brad. She knew she'd done her job well. Perhaps she was just so tired she wanted to rest.'

He put his free hand over Sally's and they sat for a moment with hands clasped on the white table-cloth. Then Brad gently dried her eyes.

'Come on, let's walk.'

He paid their bill and they moved out into the warm summer evening. They had returned to the pub beside the river and now they strolled along the towpath as a majestic harvest moon sailed above them in a blue velvet sky.

'Do you still work for Jock?' Sally had intended to guard her heart against more pain, knowing how committed she was to the children. But this big quiet man had crept under her defences. In spite of her good intentions, she was falling in love with him. Now she wanted to know everything about him.

As they walked, Brad put his arm across her shoulders which fitted comfortably against his side. He pulled her gently to him and Sally slipped her arm around his waist as they moved on, rhythmically in step.

'Jock died nearly six years ago.'

'Poor Brad. Then you were truly alone. Did he make you his heir?'

Brad's laugh held some bitterness.

'No. I told you Jock was married, although he never had much married life. Isobel, his wife, was a bit like your Dad's Sharon. She enjoyed the good things in life and wanted entertainment. She enjoyed spending Jock's money, either at her fancy apartment, or in her country mansion but never had time to join him anywhere in the world – too many social engagements, or other excuses.'

'You were very fond of Jock, weren't you?' It was clear Brad's evident dislike of Isobel stemmed from Jock's disappointment at his wife's continual absence from his side.

'Yes. The old man was good to me, almost a proper father. He was just and fair but strong-minded, something his wife and son didn't appreciate. At least, I suppose the boy didn't have much chance. Isobel kept Adrian away from his father at every opportunity. She said he wasn't strong enough for the rough and tumble of boarding school, which would have done him the world of good, or fit enough to travel with his father. I could almost forgive that if she had done it out of concern for the child, but it seemed she did it to spite Jock. I suppose she was afraid Adrian would become his father's son and she would be left out. Anyway, she dripped poison in the boy's ear from the time he was born. At last he wouldn't go anywhere near his father. That hurt the old man. He didn't show it much, but I knew him so well.'

'I'm glad you were there for him.'

Brad gave Sally's shoulders a squeeze.

'So am I. It helped I know, but I wasn't his flesh and blood so, when he died everything went to Adrian, the whole business empire Jock had built up and in which he took such pride – just as it should have done. He's Jock's blood.'

'Did he leave you nothing at all?'

'He provided generously for Isobel and everything else went to Adrian. But he had already made sure of my future. I told you, he paid me well and he gave me good advice on how to invest my money. I received bonuses for special assignments I completed and used those wisely too. Jock gave me knowledge. And knowledge is power. I was an apt pupil and listened to him. Don't worry about me, Sally. When Jock died, I was already comfortably off, and money makes money, if you know how to treat it.'

Sally laughed. 'I'm sure it does, if you do. At the end of the day I think you had the better bargain. Adrian may have got the business empire, but you had Jock's love, trust and companionship.'

Brad stopped and turned Sally to face him.

'That's more important to you, isn't it?'

'Of course. Anyone can earn money if they want to, but love and trust are precious gifts.'

Brad drew her into his arms and in the dusky intimacy of the night he claimed her lips. All the passion in Sally's generous heart was in the kiss she gave him. Brad's blood raced through his veins as he felt her surrender to him with perfect confidence. His arms tightened around her as the urge to make this woman his own filled his eager body. She was the one who could take away all the loneliness of his life. She could fill the empty void. With her he could hope for happiness. Sally would teach him to trust love and believe in future happiness.

An owl hooted as it patrolled the hedgerows and the orange moon smiled down on the embracing lovers.

Chapter Eight

Sally's happiness was plain for all to see. Her eyes sparkled and there was a buoyant spring in her step. Her friends watched and waited, sure that sometime soon there must be an interesting announcement.

Mavis Enderby, the vicar's wife, and Mrs Wilson were the only two who seemed to have any doubts as to a happy outcome. They agreed that Brad was attentive and spent all the time she would allow with Sally. They knew he never looked at another woman or sought companionship elsewhere, apart from the odd drink with Bob down at the pub, where he was becoming accepted as one of the regulars. But they looked farther. There was a certain aloofness about Brad when he was not with Sally. And who knew anything about him? Where did he come from? And, more importantly, where was he going when he was better?

This last question sometimes bothered Sally too, but she pushed it aside. If this was a Fool's Paradise then she intended to enjoy it as long as possible. But she couldn't believe the love she felt for Brad could go unrequited. It was true he hadn't said he loved her, not yet. But she knew he wanted her passionately. Several times, lately they had only just pulled back from losing themselves totally in the pleasure of each other's caresses.

Her present responsibilities would never let Sally throw caution completely to the winds. Always, even in Brad's arms with his kisses making her weak with longing and the wonderful rightness of the length of his body pressing against her, always some tiny voice of reason held her back. As soon as he sensed her slight withdrawal, reluctantly but without argument Brad would let her go free from his embrace. So for another two glorious weeks Sally lived in her happy bubble.

Then everything seemed to happen at once. With a flurry of last minute shopping the Summer holidays came to an end. The children started back to school. Brad was called to a final consultation with Peter Harrison and, while he was away, a bombshell burst on the village.

On Brad's return the new owners of the Hall were the sole topic of conversation.

'Look, Brad. There's an advertisement in the local paper for staff. They want cleaners and gardeners to start off, but it says other positions will become available. What do you think that means?' Sally barely drew breath before she was off again. She certainly didn't expect an answer. 'Apparently it's a company called Lindsey Enterprises. I've never heard of them. I wonder what they do? Perhaps it's going to be one of those Health Spas or a Conference Centre?'

Brad opened his mouth to speak but had no chance.

'Hazel says it will be a call-centre, you know, where they answer the public's questions. But I don't think that's very likely. They'd need hundreds of new telephone lines, wouldn't they, and that would cost a fortune to install at the Hall, so far away from the main road. And Mrs Wilson reckons it will be turned into an Old People's Home. That would be alright. Nice for the old folks if they do up the gardens how they were when Mrs Masterson was alive.'

It was no use. Brad couldn't get a word in edgeways and it was the same wherever he went in the village. He had to make a move and for the first time in his life he was putting it off.

Brad loved Sally. At last he had admitted it to himself, amazed how easy it had been in the end. But what he should do about it was more difficult. He knew her devotion to the children, but she deserved a future of her own, didn't she? He would have staked his life that she cared nothing for his wealth, even if she had taken in just how rich he was. But he couldn't bear the thought of it making a difference to her. He called himself every kind of fool for wanting this Summer idyll never to end. It had started out with friendship, then moved into a holiday romance and now it was deep, true love – the kind he had almost despaired of ever finding. He must tread carefully so as not to damage this treasure. Sally valued trust and honesty. What was she going to say when he confessed the facts he had been keeping from her? He screwed up his courage and resolved to confess all on Monday morning when he would have her alone at the lodge.

But on Monday morning Sally was distracted as she shook the raindrops off her jacket. The sudden shower had caught her unawares.

'Drat this weather. If I'd realised it was going to rain I'd have brought the car. Honestly! It's just one thing after another this morning.'

Realising this was not the moment to open his heart, Brad made them both a mug of coffee, sat Sally down and tried to get to the bottom of her unusual irritation.

'What's ruffled your feathers this morning?'

For a moment Sally glared at him, then grinned, and finally gave a small laugh. 'Sorry. Do I sound like a bear with a sore head? It's nothing really, just Philip playing up a bit. Three times this morning I had to correct him. You'd think he didn't know how to speak properly. But if it's not reminding him to say 'please' and 'thank you', it's insisting he ends his words properly with 't's or 'k's.'

'I shouldn't worry too much about it,' comforted Brad. 'I think it's a street cred thing. They want to sound like their mates at school.'

'But that's just the point. All his friends have been brought up to speak nicely. I know most of the mothers, and we all complain about the same thing.'

'I still say, don't worry. He'll grow out of it. I remember my Mum checking the way I spoke. Wait till he meets a girl. That'll sort him out.' Brad grinned, but Sally's answering smile was weak. She was remembering the scene that had taken place the previous evening.

'I don't have to listen to you. You're not my Mother. I don't have to do what you say.' Philip's little face had been contorted with rage as he screamed at Sally. She had simply asked him to pick up and put away his school things and suddenly he had turned into a little monster. 'I've seen you. You and Brad. They all say you're going to marry him. Then you'll leave us and I hate you,' he'd shouted finally and rushed out of the room, slamming the door. Lucy had immediately burst into tears and Sally had been torn between the two children. She had ended up giving Lucy a cuddle until she calmed down and leaving Philip until later.

Once Lucy was tucked up in bed Sally had sat down to talk quietly to Philip. He wouldn't meet her eyes and

77

she'd realised he was ashamed of his outburst. But she'd had to find a way to make the peace.

'Philip. I know I'm not your Mummy. I've never tried to be. I'm your sister, your big sister and I've tried to help Daddy look after you, that's all. You know it's hard for him having to go to work when he'd much rather be at home with you and Lucy.' There was now a definite tremble to the lower lip. Sally ploughed on, searching for just the right words. 'I'm sorry if I seem to nag you. I've never looked after younger brothers and sisters before. Until you and Lucy came along, I was all alone. I was so glad to have you. I love you both so much, but I know I get it wrong sometimes. I need you to help me.' This was too much. Sally heard a hiccough of tears and opened her arms wide to catch to her heart the bundle of miserable small boy who threw himself at her. Between the sobs the occasional word could be heard.

'Not wrong . . . sorry . . .love you too . . . didn't mean . . .'

Sally had soothed, rocked and added some of her own tears to Philip's, but she couldn't totally reassure him. If Brad asked her to, she would marry him, but where would that leave Philip and Lucy? She bit her lip.

'Penny for them. You look very pensive.'

Sally shook her head. How could she tell Brad Philip's worries when Brad had never mentioned marriage or even said he loved her? She sighed. 'Don't worry. It's just the kids.'

'Well if I can get your attention I'll try and take your mind off them.'

Sally smiled, expecting Brad to take her in his arms and kiss away the frown from her forehead. Instead he led her to the big comfortable settee and sat her down beside him, his arm around her shoulders. He gazed, unseeing, at the opposite wall and she had the feeling of déjà vu. Just so had she sat last night, choosing her words carefully to talk to Philip. Alarm bells rang in Sally's head. She sat up straighter and looked into Brad's eyes.

'Brad what is it? What's wrong? You're making me more worried, not less.' She tried to inject an amused note into her voice with pitiful results.

Brad turned to her. 'I have never, since I was twelve years old and started to work out of school hours at Jock's garage, spent so long being idle as this Summer. I know it couldn't be helped and I know I made it worse being silly and retarding my recovery, but while I have been off, things have got slack. You know I've talked to Farthing every day. She's kept me up to speed with what's been going on. At least, I think she has,' his lips twisted in a cynical smile. 'That woman sometimes takes too much on herself. I wouldn't put it past her to 'protect me' for what she believes is my own good.'

'You should be grateful she's so loyal and concerned. She didn't strike me as anyone's fool. If she didn't tell you something it must have been because you couldn't do anything about it and she would know that would upset you. Even I know that.'

Brad smiled down at Sally tucked so neatly into the hollow of his shoulder. He couldn't resist a swift kiss on her forehead, the only place he could trust himself to kiss her these days and then stop. 'My Sally. You know me very well, don't you? And I suppose you're right. I don't know what I'd do without Farthing.'

A swift stab of jealousy darted through Sally. She caught her breath.

'She's my right-hand man,' went on Brad. Sally relaxed. Surely Brad wouldn't talk about a woman he fancied in such a way? 'As I said everything's got slack without my hands on the reins. The thing is, Sally I have to go away.'

'Oh, no!' The words were out before Sally could stop herself. But she'd known Brad would have to go back to work one day, when he was better.

'I'll come back,' Brad reassured her, 'but I may be gone some time. I told you I'd invested my money and that means I have interests all over the place. I need to visit each company or factory to see everything is running smoothly. But when I come back, I promise I'll be around. I've almost decided to make Little Mithering my permanent base.'

Sally's eyes were shining. This was the solution she had dreamed about. Her, with Brad, and Dad and the children close by.

'I've never had a settled home since Mum died, just a flat where I changed my clothes and repacked my bag for the next trip. But now I think the time is right to settle down.' Brad put both arms round Sally and willingly she nestled into him, offering her lips for his kiss. He gazed at her upturned face, and she could see the need and passion in his eyes and love, surely there was love there too? 'Before I go away I want to get things right between us, Sally. There's so much I have to tell you . . . things you should understand.'

'Alright, Brad, later,' smiled Sally and pulled his head down to her waiting lips. She loved this man. Loved him and wanted to care for him and make up to him for all he had been denied as a child. She would give him so much love he would never think of his unhappiness again. She would make him forget his loneliness, wrap him in her adoration until he was at ease and comfortable with being loved so much. She would bring down the barriers she sensed in him, and he would bask in the warmth of her love and the affection of her family and friends. She would make him feel so at home he would never want to go wandering again. And in return he would let her into his heart and share his thoughts, hopes and dreams with her.

A thunderous knocking on the front door of the lodge interrupted their bliss.

'What on earth?' Brad raised his head in furious disbelief.

The banging continued. Then they heard the flap of the letterbox raised. 'Stand to there,' shouted a voice. 'Prepare to repel boarders.'

'What the . . ?' Brad sat up and ran a hand through his hair. 'I don't believe it.'

Drugged with love and passion, Sally took longer to come to her senses. 'What is it, Brad?'

'I'll have to let the maniac in, or he'll break the door down,' growled Brad, but there was a half-smile on his face.

Sally quickly sat up, pulled bra straps into place, did up her buttons and tucked her blouse into her waistband before Brad could open the door. Almost before it was ajar, a man bounded into the room. He was slight in build, but with a wiry strength, deeply tanned with sun-bleached blonde hair, bright blue eyes and the whitest teeth Sally had ever seen. These were displayed in a broad grin as he threw his arms round Brad in a bear hug.

'What do you mean by skulking down here? Farthing told me all about your little brush with the Grim Reaper. Thought you could get out of that pint you owe me, did you? And what are you doing here? I thought you were up the road?' There was a pause.

Was it Sally's imagination or did some silent message pass between the two men?

But the stranger prattled on in the same vein as before. 'Nice little nest you've got here. And pretty company too, I see,' he had at last spied Sally who was trying to make herself invisible in the depths of the big, squashy settee.

'Shut up, Chris,' commanded Brad. 'Sally. Come and meet the most disreputable man I have ever known.'

The stranger laughed. His eyes twinkled at Sally. She couldn't help but smile back.

'Not true, not true. Don't forget Horrible Harry in Colombo. And Nasty Niederholdt in Guyana.'

'OK. I'll give you those,' grinned Brad.

Sally was amazed at the transformation in the man she loved. She had never seen him so relaxed and amused. His eyes were full of laughter and affection. Who was this character Brad obviously knew so well? Why had he never mentioned him?

'Calm down, Chris. Sally, this is Christopher Melling. Chris, meet Sally Fletcher.' Brad's arm slid around Sally's waist. He pulled her to him until she rested against his side. 'Sally is my very special lady, Chris, and you will treat her with respect.' Was there a hint of warning in his voice?

'Hello, Chris.' Sally offered her hand which was taken in a firm warm grip. 'Where did you spring from?'

'From Brasil, via London and the indispensable Farthing's office. That's how I knew where to find Brad.'

'How do you two know each other?' Again there was that moment of silent communication between the two men.

'We studied engineering together and then seemed to bump into each other in outlandish places round the world.' Christopher's smile was wide and honest. Why did Sally get the impression he was feeling his way?

'That's when I was working for Jock,' put in Brad. 'I never knew where he would send me next. If it was hot, sticky, far from civilisation and extremely uncomfortable, you could bet Chris would be there too. So we used to join forces to relieve the tedium and take our minds off our misery. What brings you here now, Chris?'

'I'm on leave for four months. That's what I've accumulated while in Brasil. Then I thought I might have a change of job and scene. Perhaps find something in the UK. But it seems my plans to spend my leave with you could be scuppered. I bear missives from Farthing.'

'I was just telling Sally I must go away soon for a few weeks. Farthing's obviously used you to send me the papers I need.'

Sally felt it time to make a move. 'I'll be off and let you two talk over old times. If you're going to be around for a while Chris, you're very welcome to join us for Sunday lunch.'

Chris looked a little baffled but smiled and thanked her. Brad moved with Sally to the door.

'I'm sorry our talk was interrupted,' he smiled.

'Talk?' asked Sally with a wicked grin.

Brad laughed. 'Yes, that too.' His eyes moved over her with delight. Sally blushed, following the direction of his eyes and thoughts. 'I don't feel I can abandon Chris tonight, but can we have dinner tomorrow at our pub by the river?'

'That would be lovely. I look forward to it.' Sally held her face up for his kiss. Brad took his time to say goodbye and she was left breathless and with stars in her eyes.

As she walked home and then went about her usual tasks Sally hummed happily to herself. She was delighted Brad had a close friend. What a change this Chris person had wrought in the man Sally loved. Even when he was alone with her, Sally had sensed a certain reserve in Brad. Was that because he hadn't made up his mind to commit himself? But tomorrow all that would change. Brad had said he had things to tell her - important things, obviously - to be told in the romantic setting of the pub where they had shared their first real kiss. Sally hugged her happiness to her throughout the day and all that evening.

The following morning she sprang out of bed, got the children off to school and plated up a lunch in the fridge for her father. She sped round the cottage, making beds and tidying as she went. She could spend lunchtime and the early afternoon with Brad and do the ironing after she'd fetched Philip and Lucy from school. Then while they ate their tea she would take a long scented bath and be dressed and ready when Brad came to pick her up.

She was still smiling with pleasure at that thought when she heard the doorbell, closely followed by the opening of the front door and Brad's voice.

'Sally? Sally, are you home?'

'Brad. How lovely. I was just thinking of you.' She reached up to kiss him before she saw the frown which puckered his forehead. 'What's wrong?'

He followed her back into the roomy kitchen where the main life of the family went on. Then he put his hands on her shoulders and looked down at her. The grey of his eyes was darker today. Sally had learned that, for him, this was a sure sign of deep emotion.

'Sally darling.' Her heart thrilled. Brad was not a man who used careless endearments. 'Sally, I'm sorry. We can't have dinner tonight.' Her heart sank. So much for her romantic evening. 'I have to go away, today, now. Jim is waiting at the gate with the car. The papers Chris brought were not the ones I was waiting for, but something much more serious and needing immediate attention. I fly from Heathrow this afternoon. I'll try and keep in touch whenever I can. But don't fret if some time passes and you don't hear from me. Even mobile phone signals are dodgy in the jungle, or if they're cut off by a range of mountains,' he smiled ruefully.

'There was so much I wanted to tell you, make you understand, explain to you, before I had to leave you, but there's no time. Tell me, Sally. Do you trust me?'

Sally frowned. What a strange question. 'You know I do, Brad. Why do you ask?'

He bit his lip. 'Damn this trip. It couldn't have come at a worse time. Look, Sally. While I'm away you may hear things . . . learn things . . . which confuse you, things you may not like. Just believe I would never do anything to hurt you and trust me, please?'

'Brad, I don't understand. You're frightening me.'

Brad cursed again. 'I'm doing this all wrong. But there's no time. I'm sorry darling, but I have to go.' His eyes searched her face hungrily. He pulled her into his arms and held her tightly against him as if to imprint her body on his own for ever. Then he moved her away from him, looked into her eyes and spoke quietly with deep sincerity.

'I love you, Sally Fletcher. Always remember, I love you.' He kissed her forehead gently and turned away.

Sally followed him to the door and watched him stride down the path to the waiting car. As he opened its rear door he turned towards her. 'Any problems, you can trust Chris. He'll be around for a bit. Bye Sally. I'll be back. I promise.'

Tears blinded Sally as the big, black car drove away down the village street.

Chapter Nine

Sally's happiness was shattered. She had looked forward to the evening with such glad anticipation. Disappointment sat like a black dog on her shoulders. She moved through the day in a fog of misery. The final straw came as she returned from Brownies to find Bob sitting reading the paper. He looked up as she came through the door.

'Brad rang, love.' Sally's face lit up. 'There was no-one home, but he left a message on the Ansaphone. He said sorry to miss you. Don't forget what he said, and he'll call again if he can.' Sally hurried to the telephone. 'Don't bother, pet. I've already wiped the tape clean.'

Sally stood still, with eyes closed, as the tears threatened to choke her. How could he? How could Dad have taken Brad's message from her? She longed to hear his voice.

Bob looked more closely at his eldest child. 'Sal? What's wrong, pet? Brad said he'd phone again. Why don't you pop round there? I'll see to the children.' He put down his paper and came to where Sally was fighting for control. 'What is it girl?'

Sally shook her head, helplessly. 'I can't pop round, Dad. Brad's gone.'

Bob Fletcher's face tightened. His eyes were grim. 'You mean he's left you?'

'No. Not left me. He was called away.' She gulped back the tears which threatened to choke her as she explained. 'He's coming back, but I don't know when and we didn't have time to talk and we were going out tonight for a special evening and he said there was something special he had to say to me and now he can't and I miss him already.' The words tumbled out in a rush. 'I just wanted to hear his voice Daddy,' she wailed.

The childhood name showed Bob more than anything how small and hurt Sally felt. He pulled her into his arms to hug her close and she wept hot tears down the front of his shirt. As he patted her shoulder and soothed her with kindly murmurs, she let all the tension and disappointment flood out. She had kept control of herself, her emotions, her sacrifices and the hopes and fears of this little family for so long without realising what a toll it had taken on her own reserves of strength and courage. Now the floodgates opened out of all proportion to present events. Somehow Bob sensed something of this, but it was the pathetic plea for a sound of Brad's voice which tore at his heart.

After the death of Sally's mother, Bob would have given all he possessed to hear her voice once more. So he cuddled his grown-up daughter and cursed himself for having erased Brad's message.

When the children heard Brad had gone away, they acted predictably. Lucy's bottom lip stuck out in dismay. She demanded when her big friend would be returning. Philip's eyes grew huge and troubled. Sally knew those signs and was able to reassure him Brad hadn't left because of Philip's outburst and Brad would come back. Unfortunately she couldn't say when. Brad had at last said he loved her but then he had gone. As time went by the lonely days unrolled like a ship's wake trailing back into a happier past.

Sally stayed away from the lodge. It was all very well for Brad to say, trust Chris, but Sally associated the new arrival with Brad's departure and had no wish to pursue the acquaintance. She snatched the mail each morning with eager hands but, mostly, she was disappointed. There was a card posted at Heathrow, then one from New York, another missed telephone call from Denver, and then nothing.

Sally lost weight. She tried to busy herself each day but had become so used to running the house and family it required little or no mental effort. Her worried father watched her gaze into space for long minutes. Sometimes a tender smile tugged at the corners of her mouth as she relived happy memories, but all too often her shoulders drooped and her expression was desolate as she longed for Brad's return. At last Bob had a brainwave.

'Don't you think it's time you put your plan into action?'

'What plan?' Sally asked disinterestedly.

'Weren't you going to take on some more clients this autumn?'

Sally thought about it. That had been her idea. Brad's arrival had put it out of her mind but now she had so much spare time it would be good to fill it with work she enjoyed. She mentioned her availability to Major Lawson and Fred Tucker who had been so anxious she should work for their friends. But it seemed the friends had got fixed up with satisfactory people, so Sally had to look elsewhere. It was while she was searching the local paper for its business address that she saw the advertisement which provided the answer to her needs. Lindsey Enterprises, the new owners of the Hall, were looking for a part-time bookkeeper. It wasn't quite the job Sally would have chosen, but the advantage of working so close to home couldn't be disregarded. She phoned for an appointment and wondered what she would find at the Hall.

It was a beautiful autumn day when Sally presented herself for the interview, neatly dressed in the kind of business suit she used to wear to the office in Libchester. As she had walked through the Home Park the exercise had brought a touch of colour to cheeks, which had lately grown pale through lack of sleep and unhappiness. She mounted the two shallow steps which separated the pillared portico from the gravel sweep in front of the lovely old house and rang the bell. The big oak doors stood open to a vestibule where a beautiful arrangement of chrysanthemums stood on a side table. Sally was admiring them when the half-glassed inner door opened.

The small grey-haired woman who greeted her was pleasant and businesslike. Having enquired her name, she looked at Sally with eyes which seemed to take in every detail of her appearance and even look into her mind and assess her personality. Then she held out her hand in invitation.

'Good morning, Sally Fletcher. I am Athena Penney. Please come this way.'

She led Sally across the shining parquet floor of the hall and into a sunlit room which may once have been the library of the house, but which now also housed a bank of computers, a photocopier, a fax machine and a large desk on which stood three telephones.

'Do sit down. Would you like coffee?'

Sally accepted the offer but was inwardly frowning. There was something about Athena Penney's voice. What was it? They'd never met, she was sure of that, but surely she'd hear that voice before? No matter. She must concentrate on her interview. The other woman was holding the cv. Sally had sent in. Once they had been served coffee by one of the village women Sally recognised with a smile, the interview began.

When Miss Penney remarked how overqualified Sally was for the position, Sally had to explain her reasons for wanting a job which would keep her close to the village. She simply said she was helping her father bring up her younger brother and sister and left it at that. The rest was no-one else's business. Miss Penney seemed delighted Sally could join them, offered her three mornings work each week at a reasonable salary and asked if Sally had any questions.

'What exactly is Lindsey Enterprises? And for whom would I be working?' Sally was delighted at being able to ask the questions the whole village had been pondering since the first advertisement appeared.

'Lindsey Enterprises is the holding company for a wide range of interests. It is privately owned, and we expect to make the Hall our new administrative headquarters at least for the next few years. You will be answerable to me and if you have any problems or queries don't be afraid to ask. Initially you will set up a simple system for the household expenditure. I am now resident here, and in the future there will probably be others and a larger staff. Wages and daily budgeting will come into that. Also the repair and redecoration of the house together with some structural alteration will all come out of the same budget.' Miss Penney gazed at the window for a moment, but Sally had the impression the other woman saw nothing of the formal garden outside, where two men were busy bringing order out of years of neglect. 'Having seen your excellent qualifications, it may be possible, in the future that I shall ask you to do some more interesting work. Have you ever been involved in investigative accounting?'

Sally smiled. 'Yes. I'd done about a year of that kind of work when I had to come home to look after the children. I really enjoyed it, playing detective.'

'Exactly. Well, we'll see what happens. I'll show you where you will be working.'

She led Sally to the left-hand end of the wide hall which cut the house in two and opened the door of a smaller room. Perhaps it had been a butler's pantry or servants' sitting room, as it was quite near the kitchen quarters, but now it was simply furnished as a functional office. There was a window which gave onto the front of the house, and a small cloakroom next door.

Miss Penney led Sally farther on down to the end of the hall.

'You can use this door when you come to work. As we have so few staff at the moment, I keep the inner front door locked. It is easier if we stick to this side entrance. I look forward to seeing you on Monday, Sally.' She shook Sally's hand once more and ushered her out.

It was only when Sally was half way home she realised she was not much wiser as to the nature of the business Lindsey Enterprises conducted, or why they had chosen to come to the depths of the country.

On Monday morning Sally began her new job. She met the rest of the staff; one live-in elderly cook-housekeeper, Miss Penney had brought down from London and a switchboard operator who came each day from Libchester. The rest were locals who worked in the house and garden, cleaning and polishing and also painting and decorating. Occasionally a dashing sports car swept up the main drive and a red-haired girl stalked through the rooms giving orders and making notes. She was, apparently, a talented designer and restoration expert bringing the old house back to its former glory, but Sally had little to do with her.

She saw Miss Penney each day at work and was impressed with her calm efficiency. Sally soon knew everyone at the Hall by name and found they all addressed Athena Penney formally. Sally could understand that. The older woman was perfectly friendly but with a certain reserve. Instinctively Sally found herself thinking of her boss as Miss Penney and almost forgot the Christian name she had been told. She enjoyed her new job and only wished she could spend more time there, where she could lose herself in figures and hold her anxious thoughts at bay. But with every day that passed without news of Brad, Sally's vivid imagination tended more and more to dwell on what awful things could happen in the wild, untamed country he and Chris had spoken about.

One lunchtime, as she closed the door of her comfortable office and turned to go home, she saw the dim figure of a man at the far end of the long hall. As he walked away from her, a beam of light came through an open doorway and struck his bleached blonde hair. Sally turned back to have a second look, but he had gone. She shook her head. It must have been a trick of the light. What possible reason would Christopher Melling have to come to the offices of Lindsey Enterprises?

Another day as she gazed idly out of her window, while her brain formulated the answer to a problem on the desk before her, she saw the back view of someone striding down the drive in the distance. It couldn't be him. Just someone like him. But thinking about Christopher renewed her longing for Brad.

There was an aching wound in her heart which could only be cured by his return. Each night she slept with all she had of him tucked inside her pillowcase, the two postcards from America, the short letter from London and the card which had arrived with her flowers. Such little treasures, but they meant so much.

She held his letter against her cheek. His hand had held it. His strong, decisive writing had formed the message it held for her. Writing so like the writer. She'd close her eyes and see his face smiling down at her with that special warmth in his eyes, those grey eyes which changed colour with his emotions. She'd never known there were so many shades of grey. She felt again the strength of his arms, the feel of his body pressed close to hers, his unique smell of tangy aftershave, freshly laundered linen and his own male essence. She relived the caress of his hands and the warmth of his lips, moving so passionately on her own. No-one knew how many silent tears dripped onto Sally's pillow. If only he would phone again, or send a letter? But the silence grew longer.

At last, in despair, Sally went to the Gate Lodge where Christopher Melling greeted her with delight.

'Sally. I've been meaning to find out where you live and come to call. I haven't forgotten your invitation to Sunday lunch. My tummy rumbles whenever I think of the roast beef of Old England. Are we still on?'

Sally was taken aback. She'd forgotten she'd invited him, over a month ago. It had been as Brad's guest of course. But her good manners couldn't refuse him now.

'Of course. I suppose you didn't get much beef in Brasil? Or am I wrong? No, it's Argentina, isn't it where they have so much beef? I'm confused. I know so little about South America,' she babbled. 'But I really came to ask if you had any idea where Brad might be?' Did she imagine a shutter came down behind his eyes?

'Brad? Well, he could be anywhere. I mean he's doing the rounds isn't he?'

'That was his original plan. But whatever you brought down to him changed his mind. He went off in a hurry on some special trip. I'd ask Farthing if only I knew her telephone number. She's his right-hand man, as it were. She must know where he's gone.'

'I shouldn't worry too much, if I were you. It's not as though it's the first time he's been out of touch for so long.'

'Really?'

'Good heavens, yes. Some of the mining camps where we've met in the past are way out at the back end of nowhere. Transportation by mule or shanks's pony, weeks to get there and then more weeks to get back again. No radio signals or telephone lines. We once thought of setting up a carrier pigeon service, but the eagles would have eaten the poor little things.'

Sally couldn't help laughing at Chris's cheery nonsense. For the moment at least, his breezy assurances stilled the worst of her fears.

On the following Sunday he joined the Fletcher family for lunch, entertained the children with wonderful conjuring tricks, and accompanied Bob down to the pub in the evening. His visit was a great success and was repeated more and more frequently in the following weeks.

Sally enjoyed his company because he knew Brad. She asked nothing better than to hear tales of their adventures together. If all Chris said could be believed, he and Brad had shared hair-raising adventures with the panache and daring of storybook heroes and left a string of brokenhearted beauties in their wake. Sally took all this with a large pinch of salt but found her heart lighter in Chris's company. Surely, if only half he had told her was true, Brad was simply on a long trek in difficult terrain. He would be in touch as soon as he could. In Chris's company she found it easier to keep cheerful but at the end of the day she lay awake, longing for Brad and wondering where in all the world he could be? Was he alright? Or ill? If only she had some idea where he'd gone. She sent up many urgent prayers for his safety and hugged to her heart the love he had professed for her. 'Trust me' he'd said. 'I'll come back. I love you.'

In the meantime Chris proved an undemanding and amusing friend. When Sally realised he was serious about staying in the area and finding at least a semi-permanent home, she offered him her flat in Libchester. Her repentant agent had managed to get rid of the revolting Clarks before the end of the lease and the flat was now vacant.

Once Chris had seen it, he declared himself delighted and planned to move in as soon as Brad returned to claim the Lodge. Before then however Sally wanted to completely redecorate and in this she found a willing helper. Many companionable hours were spent painting and papering and always with an undertone of good humoured chat and teasing.

Sally barely noticed when Chris laid an arm across her shoulders as they walked along. Sometimes he would catch her hand in his and swing them together. He was always laughing and teasing, so Sally looked upon him as an extra brother, quite sure he realised her commitment to Brad, his friend. It wasn't until Chris took her firmly in his arms and tried to kiss her goodnight, after a pleasant evening out, that she was shocked into realisation of his feelings towards her.

'No. No. Chris. What are you doing?'

Chris was puzzled. 'Don't you like me, Sally? I thought we were getting on well together.'

'Of course I like you, Chris. But I love Brad. He's your friend. Surely you can't believe I'd cheat on him?'

Chris shook his head. 'Hang on a minute Sally. Love's a big word. Brad's had girlfriends before. Most of them are still his friends. I'm sure he's never hurt anyone, but commitment? No. Not our Brad. I've never known a guy so light-hearted in his love affairs. He likes women, but he never gives his heart, my dear. Believe me, I know.' Chris's eyes were kind as he looked at Sally, then his expression changed, became more serious.

'I thought I was the same, but you, Sally Fletcher, you've changed my mind. The more I see you, the more I want to know you.' He put his hands on Sally's shoulders and looked gravely into her eyes. His sincerity was clear. 'I think I'm falling in love with you, Sally.'

The ready tears sprang to Sally's eyes. These days they never seemed far away. She blinked them back impatiently. 'You can't Chris. You mustn't. I don't want to hurt you.'

'And I don't want Brad to hurt you, sweet Sally. But I'm afraid he will if you give him your heart.'

'Then it's too late. He's already got it. He took it with him.' And the tears fell in earnest. Chris tried to comfort her. She couldn't believe Brad had not been serious. Surely Chris was wrong? She struggled out of the circle of his arms. 'What did you mean when you said he never committed himself? Surely if you say you love someone that's a commitment?'

97

'Exactly. That's a word Brad would never use. He could be attracted to someone, like them, be fond of them, appreciate them, but he'd never tell a woman he loved her. It's a sort of thing with him. He said once that people undervalue love. In one of our more serious moments,' Chris added with a smile.

'There you are then. He did say he loved me. And he promised to come back. So doesn't that mean something?'

'Did he really say that? I had no idea. We were only together for a few hours before he left. He said you were special at that first meeting, but I'm afraid I took that as a friendly warning not to move in on you.'

'But that's just what you've done.'

'No. That was before we knew he would be going away. We often used to pinch each other's girls. It didn't matter. I told you there were no deep feelings involved, and if a girl found she liked me better than Brad, or the other way around, well all's fair in love and war. It used to be a sort of game. That's all I thought he meant, but this changes everything. Lucky old Brad. If he really does love you, Sally, he'll never do anything to hurt you. You can be sure of that.'

Sally smiled through the tears which stuck on her lashes like raindrops on a hedgerow. 'Thank you, Chris. But he is hurting me by his silence. Do you really think he's alright?'

Chris was silent, looking at Sally with a slight frown on his face, deep in thought.

'Look. I'll ring around a few mates. Perhaps someone'll have news of him,' he said at last.

With that Sally had to be satisfied. She was worried at first that Chris's revelation of his feelings might change their friendship. That would have been a pity as she had come to rely on his company as a sort of link to Brad. But there was a subtle alteration in Chris's attitude. She still saw him almost daily, but he became more the big brother she needed than the lover he would like to have been.

At work Sally found her tasks easy and the people she came into contact with were pleasant. It was an undemanding job until one Tuesday morning when she was called into Miss Penney's office. The older woman looked strained but greeted Sally with her usual pleasant smile.

'Ah, Sally, come in. Sit down. You probably remember I proposed using your talents in a more demanding role on our first meeting?' Sally nodded. 'Well, if you are willing, the time has now come. I have here the books of a small company we acquired about two years ago.' She hesitated a moment then continued. 'The Chairman of Lindsey Enterprises has had his suspicions for some time that financially something wasn't right. Not much you could put your finger on, small discrepancies, mistakes which, when they came to light, were written off as genuine errors, that kind of thing. But now we have received a definite lead.

'In the small hours of this morning our people raided the offices of this company and seized all the paperwork. I do mean all the paperwork, I'm afraid, Sally.' Miss Penney gestured to the far side of her office where a large number of the cardboard boxes used for storing files were stacked against the wall. 'Also their computer discs. You said you liked to play detective so now is your chance. I appreciate this is much more specialised work and, of course, your pay will reflect that fact. Also I should be obliged if it were possible for you to give us more hours.

This matter is quite urgent and the more time you can give to it, the better.'

'Wouldn't it be simpler to bring in more staff?'

'Simpler, yes. I agree. But this whole exercise is extremely sensitive and highly confidential. If any rumour of what we are doing got out, the share price would go through the floor. Also, the guilty parties might escape and that wouldn't do. That wouldn't do at all.'

Sally was surprised how grim Miss Penney looked. It was almost as if she took this fraud personally, if fraud it was.

'But surely they'll know what's happening?'

Miss Penney allowed herself a smile. 'We have leaked the fact that the VAT people have made a snap inspection. The rotten apples in this barrel believe themselves quite safe against such a specific investigation.' Her face looked grim. 'He thinks himself untouchable. I warn you, Sally, they have been clever. You'll need all your wits about you to unravel their schemes. And . . . needless to say it, but I will . . . this is absolutely confidential. Tell no-one what you are doing, no-one at all.'

Sally left Miss Penney's office with something of the old spring in her step. At last something to get her teeth into. All the paperwork would be put into her office which had a new Yale lock fitted. She and Miss Penney were the only people with keys. Sally should come and go whenever she could manage a few extra hours, most probably in the evenings, when Dad would be home for the children.

Bob Fletcher was just grateful Sally had cheered up and was taking more interest in life than she had since Brad's departure. In answer to his queries she murmured the magic word 'audit'. He remembered what a busy time of year it used to be for Sally's firm when auditing the books of their clients and was satisfied she needed to do the extra work.

As she got stuck into her new challenge Sally found there were hours at a stretch when she didn't think about Brad. Work was a great antidote to worry.

Chapter Ten

'Sally. Sally.'

Brad tried to call her name. But no sound came out. Yet in his head he was yelling. If only he could make her hear, he knew she would come to him. Sally. His Sally, with her sparkling eyes and warm generous mouth. How could he have let her go? At last he had found the woman of his dreams, a woman he had hardly dared let himself believe could be real. And then what? He held back. Afraid of commitment? Or afraid she couldn't be as wonderful as she seemed? Too afraid to put it to the test. He should have wrapped her in his arms and never let go.

He rolled his head in anguish as tears of weakness slipped from beneath his eyelids and slid down his cheeks. Sally, I need you. You're the one who can make sense of this whole world. I'm lost. I don't know where I am or what's happening, but if I can hold on to you everything will be alright. Where are you Sally? Forgive me, my darling. Come to me now. I need you so much. Oh, Sally. I love you.

Then the hot darkness closed in again.

Someone had rolled Brad's eyeballs in sand. He tried to blink it away, but the lids weighed a ton. His head was cracking and there was a rotten smell in his nostrils. He lay still and tried to gather his thoughts. Occasionally a shiver rippled over his body and from somewhere came a clattering noise he found very irritating. Desperately he tried to make sense of his position. What could he remember? Heat, dreadful heat. He'd been burning up. Then Sally had come and laid her hand on his forehead. She raised his head and gave him a bitter drink. It tasted foul but she wouldn't let him turn his head away. Afterwards he'd gone to sleep. But before that? There'd been a boat. No. A canoe. He could still feel the blow as his body hit the hollowed-out wood. He struggled to get his thoughts in order. It had been so hot. But then why was he shivering? At last he realised the noise which bothered him was the chattering of his teeth. He groaned and tried to reach for the bedcovers but only touched his own body which seemed clad in some sodden material. Brad gave up and drifted back to sleep.

Some time later he felt Sally's hand on his forehead again. This time he managed to open his eyes, desperate to see her face. But it wasn't Sally. An old brown-skinned woman bent over him. She smiled as his eyes opened. Her few remaining teeth were stained and crooked. She had a piece of bone inserted by way of ornament through one nostril and her ear lobes hung long beside her neck, weighed down by massive copper rings. Brad blinked and wondered if he was dreaming. But the apparition was still there. She stood up and said something to a small girl almost hidden behind her. Brad saw the big questioning eyes and thought of Lucy.

When the little one had reappeared with some sort of container, Brad was helped to swallow the bitter concoction he half remembered from before. He smiled at the memory of his mother telling him all medicines tasted nasty but did you good. He hoped she was right. At his smile the old woman cackled with approval and called over her shoulder.

Brad looked round. He was in some kind of native hut. Soon it was crowded as more and more women pushed in to look at the strange white man. Two strong, younger women began to undress Brad. He tried to protest, unwilling to provide a peep show for the interested spectators, but he was too weak to argue. As his clothes were pulled off him, he realised the disgusting smell in his nostrils came from his own body and the sodden remnants of his shirt and trousers. Stale sweat, vomit, blood and dear knows what. He didn't want to think about it.

Once he was naked the women bathed him with soft clothes then poured fresh water over him. This ran off his body and through the plaited mattress on which he lay, to be absorbed by the ground beneath. His mattress was woven on a frame supported a few inches above the ground, no doubt to let any possible breeze cool the occupant. Once he was clean his body dried quickly in the heat and then he was wrapped in a cotton sarong and left to sleep.

The next time he woke he felt almost himself and he was hungry. As if she knew this his old nurse appeared with a bowl of broth. It was to be the first of many meals Brad ate without letting himself enquire too closely what was in it. All he cared about was regaining his strength and getting in touch with Sally.

Gradually he was strong enough to stand up and go outside the hut to relieve himself. He found his was one of many huts in a village beside the river. His friends or captors, as yet he didn't know which, made him a hammock slung between two trees. There he spent many hours getting stronger and amusing the small children with funny faces and childish tricks with a pliable piece of liana which he used as string. He drank and ate whatever was given to him and felt no threat from the smiling faces which surrounded him. But he was desperate to escape.

One evening he lay in his hammock and idly looked up at the moon. Was Sally looking too? If he sent her his love by moon-post, would she feel it reach her? He smiled at his fancies. He'd never been a romantic or particularly imaginative lover. But then he'd never loved anyone as he loved Sally.

He recalled every meeting, every conversation they'd ever had. It had been so simple, the way she had become a part of his life. It was true the time spent at the Gate Lodge hadn't been his usual life, far from it. Was that why he had welcomed Sally into his heart? Had the long weeks of inactivity lowered his guard, made him more trusting? Looking back now, that whole episode was like a fairy story. A pang shot through Brad as he wondered for one brief second if Sally, Little Mithering and the weeks he had spent there had all been part of his illness? Had he dreamed of Sally's smile, her kiss, the feel of her body melting into his arms? Was it all part of his delirium? Please God, no. He went back over details, desperately trying to reassure himself that his love for Sally was reality and not some beautiful dream. With his limited experience of perfect trust and love, he could never have imagined anyone like Sally. He pushed away the horrid doubts which had plagued him. Sally was there, waiting for him to return as he had promised. He cursed his weakness and enforced idleness as he lay so far away from her. Did she think he'd forgotten her? Did she think he'd broken his promise? As he gazed at the heavens Brad realised the moon was almost full. But that couldn't be right?

His memory of events before he woke in the hut was gradually returning. There'd been a message brought by a small boy. He'd followed the child to the rendezvous and lifted his head to look at the full moon suspended overhead. Perhaps he owed his life to that movement as the blow, which felled him, only glanced off his skull. He had never quite lost consciousness; had been aware of being lifted, carried and then dropped into the canoe, which was pushed off from the bank, to be carried far downstream, away from the scene of the intended murder. No doubt they had then dealt with his jeep, which was parked at the roadhouse.

But the moon had been full and here it was, nearly full again. That could only mean he had been here for a whole month. He vaguely remembered lying in the bottom of the canoe in the baking heat of the sun and later being eaten alive by the mosquitoes.

His travels had taken him so speedily from one country to another, he was sure the various medications he had armed himself with hadn't had time to take effect. And his usual immunity had been lost during the long Summer months at the Gate Lodge. His latest stop on the trail he followed had been in Asuncion. From there he had gone by train and jeep deep into the interior, never quite sure if he was in Paraguay or Argentina. Even in these modern days, this was a mosquito infested area. It was clear to him now that these natives had rescued him from death in the canoe and tended him through a nasty bout of malaria.

As he made sense of the immediate past, he was sure his rescuers were not in league with his would-be assassins, but he didn't know how to communicate with them. Smiles and nods were all very well to show friendship and thanks, but how could he ask for transport to the nearest large town or village?

He had to get away; back to civilisation, Sally, and retribution. He could now walk unaided around the compound. But any time he attempted to follow one of the trails leading away from the camp, he was prevented, kindly but firmly. It made sense Brad knew. He had no idea where he was or what dangers might lurk in the thick foliage beyond the clearing, but it also meant he was not free to move about. Out of consideration for his welfare? Or because someone had ordered it? Was he getting paranoid? Small wonder when he thought about the previous weeks and months. Brad was certain this was the second time he had nearly been murdered and he didn't feel like waiting here for the third and, maybe finally successful, attempt.

One day when he had already begun to form ludicrous escape plans a hubbub of sound from the direction of the river drew all the villagers on the run. Brad followed more slowly. He had wondered at the absence of menfolk in the village and now he saw the reason why. A veritable fleet of canoes was being dragged up onto the riverbank. And here were the men, of all ages. Some were already unloading bales of cloth, cooking pots and sacks, no doubt containing food unavailable in the forest. But it was the centre and largest of the canoes which drew Brad's attention. In it sat a white man. Brad tensed. He felt his heart beat faster and clenched his fists. Was this friend or foe? He waited where he stood, totally vulnerable. With no weapon or means to defend himself he was helpless as the stranger was helped ashore and led up to him.

The other man was short and stocky with blonde hair cut very short. He had vivid blue eyes and the sun caught the golden hairs on the backs of his tanned hands. But the smile and outstretched hand did little to allay Brad's suspicion. His enemy would hardly come and bash him over the head again in front of so many witnesses, would he?

'Klaus Fulner,' the newcomer introduced himself. 'Your hosts came to tell me you were in a spot of bother.' He spoke excellent English with a light, pleasant German accent. 'They come to see me for medicines on occasion, although usually they are pretty good at curing themselves. It's only for the diseases we wretched Europeans have introduced to their country that they need our help in treating them. I'm actually doing a three-year study of native medicines and the plants they use. We can learn so much from the indigenous population. But I mustn't get on my hobby-horse and bore you now. How can I help?' He smiled, the wide ingenuous smile of a young child.

Brad relaxed a little, shook the offered hand and introduced himself.

'I think I have been dosed with a native remedy for malaria. It tasted disgusting but must have done the trick. I'm feeling great now, just a bit wobbly. But I really need to get back to civilisation and make contact with my office.'

Klaus Fulner gave Brad one penetrating look but didn't ask any awkward questions. 'No problem. Just hang on until I've had a quick check on these good people, then you can come downstream with me.'

He was as good as his word. Brad had nothing to pack. His clothes had fallen apart when the village women tried to wash them. The pockets had been empty, and his wristwatch gone when he came to his senses. There had been nothing left to identify his body. When he said goodbye to his rescuers, he wore the clean sarong he had been given that morning. He had nothing to give them, only his thanks.

'That's all they need' assured Klaus. 'They are gentle people, with simple needs, but they can tell when you are being genuine. They offered you help and friendship. That you give your thanks and friendship in return is enough.'

Brad felt humble as he sat in the canoe and looked one last time at the clearing where his life had been given back to him. He would never forget.

Then he turned his head and looked to the future, which held Sally. His heart lifted at the thought of holding her again in his arms and hearing her dear voice tease him. He longed to fly to her side and make her his own. He'd never let her go again.

But before he could do that there were ugly facts to be dealt with. When he claimed Sally at last, he must be sure he brought no threat to her safety with him. While his enemy worked underground, anyone dear to Brad would be at risk. It had taken Brad and those he employed, many tedious and frustrating weeks to track down the opposition and now they were so close to victory. His enemy thought him dead and might get careless. So, for the moment, Brad should remain dead.

Sally turned the envelope over in her hand and frowned. Who could be writing to her from Australia and with a typed address? Laughing at herself, she slit it open and withdrew a postcard. As she turned it over she gasped, then bit her lip with joy to stop the foolish tears. Brad. His dear writing. She would know it anywhere. Eagerly she read the message, then frowned. What on earth was he talking about? No greeting, no signature, no names anywhere; just a cryptic message.

'I'm playing little sister's favourite game with a face like her brother's at the crease. Play your own cards.'

Sally turned the card over and over. The picture showed a golf course at a place called Kukup, in Malaysia. The stamp and frank on the envelope were from Australia. Was Brad there? What did the message mean? It didn't make sense. But Brad would know she longed to hear from him. He wouldn't write rubbish unless there was a good reason. She looked again at the words on the card, tried to break them down to give a meaning.

Little sister must mean Lucy. Her favourite game was hide-and-seek. She loved it and Brad had often joined in. 'Her brother' was Philip. The crease? Of course. A cricket crease. Sally smiled. It was always the same when Philip took his place. He would hold his bat just so, 'middle and leg', he would say, or something else like that, with such a serious little face. Serious. Was that it? Was that what Brad meant? And the rest. 'Your own cards', presumably Sally's cards. But what cards? Birthday? Christmas? Sally racked her brains but couldn't make sense of it at all. She looked back at the other words. Brad was playing hide-and-seek and it was serious. Her heart beat faster. Did this mean Brad was in danger, running away from something or someone? If only he would come home, he could be safe. She would protect him, she and Dad and Chris. Chris.

For a moment Sally thought her problem solved. She could ask Chris. He and Brad were so close perhaps Chris would know what Brad meant? But then she paused. If Brad needed Chris or wanted help from him, he would surely contact him at the Lodge? She would wait and see if Chris heard from Brad before blurting out her news. As it was, she was going to be late for work.

Sally waded her way meticulously through yet another pile of invoices, matching entries and checking for any discrepancy however small. She sighed. So far, there had been nothing to point to any funny business in this little Import/Export company. Everything seemed to be above board. She stretched up and pulled back her shoulders, rolling her head around to loosen the kinks.

At that moment Athena Penney walked into the room and smiled at her. 'Getting cramped are you? I know it's a thankless kind of job, but very important I assure you. Come and have a cup of coffee and a walk round the garden. You'll find it will blow the cobwebs away and you'll be able to concentrate better afterwards. It's no good trying too hard and missing something. You've just got to have patience.'

Patience. The word leapt out at Sally as though bathed in neon lights. That's what Brad meant. She must have patience. Her own cards. Cards on her own. Patience. She'd cracked it.

Her smile was so wide and brilliant Miss Penney thought Sally must have been truly despairing, but Sally hugged her new knowledge to herself for the rest of the day and all the way home.

She had heard from Brad and he had sent her a message to be patient. It was enough, for now.

Chapter Eleven

Now Sally had heard from Brad she tried her hardest not to fret. During the day she concentrated on her work and the children's needs and chatter, firmly pushing thoughts of Brad away. This proved difficult when Lucy would ask so often when her big friend Brad was coming home.

At work Sally found it easier to control her wandering thoughts. Finally, there seemed to be a pattern emerging in the paper chase she was following. It was a pattern which shouldn't have been there and one of which she had high hopes. Eagerly she hurried to work each morning and tried to find the next step in her journey through a very cleverly constructed maze. She tried to come back in the evenings as often as possible. Anything was better than gazing into space, missing Brad, and worrying if he was safe.

She had received two more postcards sent in the same way as the first, but one was from Sri Lanka and the other from Canada. Either Brad was jetting around the world fast enough to make his head spin, or he was getting other people to post his mail. The last thought made Sally worry even more and all the postcards said in his strong well-formed handwriting were the two words, 'Keep playing'. She assumed, and hoped, it meant keep on being patient. And she tried to. Brad had asked her to trust him and she would; she did. But it was so hard not knowing what was happening. Was all this cloak and dagger stuff really necessary? And if so, why? At this point she wrenched her thoughts away from pursuing such an agonising path. She could drive herself mad that way.

Sally wasn't a natural liar, so she found it difficult to keep Dad and the kids in the dark. With relief, Bob Fletcher had noticed a change in his eldest child. When he asked Sally why she seemed so much more content, less nervous and unhappy, she shrugged off the question.

'I've decided to be sensible, Dad. I can't make anything good happen by worrying. Brad asked me to trust him, and I will. I'm sure he'd be here if he could.'

'Good girl,' Bob smiled and patted Sally's shoulder. 'Well done. He'll be proud of you when he gets back and finds how well you've coped.'

Her father's praise made Sally feel like a fraud, but she remembered Brad's words. This was serious, not a game at all and so she kept silent.

She tried to avoid Chris who knew how unhappy she'd been when no word came from Brad. But one evening he arrived at the cottage unexpectedly. She answered the door to his knock.

'Hi, Sally,' he greeted her, with a kiss on the cheek and a searching look into her eyes. 'Long time, no see. How's tricks? Heard from Brad yet?'

Sally turned away, as though to lead him into the kitchen, but really to hide the blush she was sure was staining her cheeks. Without a downright lie, how could she answer? Inspiration came to her aid. She put an eager expression on her face and turned back to Chris, clapping her hands as if in excitement.

'You've heard from him? Oh, Chris. How wonderful. Where is he? When's he coming home? Why didn't he call? Do tell me all about him. Where is he?' She bombarded Chris with questions so fast and furious he was taken aback. At last he managed to catch her hands and shush her.

'No, Sally. No. I haven't heard from him. I asked if you had. I'm sorry. I didn't mean to get your hopes up like that. Obviously you haven't had word either. I did as I promised you. I contacted some of our mutual friends, phoned around some of the places we've stayed in the past in different countries, but nothing. Don't worry. No news is good news, isn't that what they say?'

Sally let her shoulders slump and hung her head. She was only too happy to hide her face from Chris. She felt dreadful, deceiving him this way. But surely if Brad had wanted Chris to know where he was, he would telephone him? She was glad she hadn't blurted it all out when the first card arrived, but she wished she knew what was going on.

The following week another card arrived for Sally, this time from Singapore. She kissed Brad's handwriting and hid the card with the others inside her pillowcase. By now she had stopped worrying quite so much about his safety. He could obviously get his mail posted all over the place, so he must have friends working with him. He wasn't alone and that must be good. As long as the cards kept arriving, Sally would keep up her spirits and look forward to his homecoming. She must be special to him as she was the only one he had got in touch with. She hugged the knowledge to her. He'd said he loved her only once. But if he meant it, then surely once was enough?

She spent many happy hours lying in bed, imagining just how it would be when Brad came home. She imagined the light in his eyes and felt the strength of his arms as they went around her, pulling her body close to his. She stroked

114

his face and traced every beloved feature, following the curve of his mobile eyebrows, then across the lids above the grey eyes, so dark in passion. She cupped his cheek in her hand then trailed her fingers along the firm line of his jaw. When they reached his mouth, he would kiss each finger as she drew them over his warm lips until, unable to wait a moment longer, he claimed her own lips in a kiss which would bind them together for ever. Hugging her pillow in her arms, Sally would fall asleep, with a happy smile on her face.

One morning, seated at her desk Sally's eyes lit up with a beam of triumph. Carefully she checked the figures and invoices in front of her. There was no mistake. She'd found the pattern. She knew now how it had been done. Money had been siphoned out of the company, reducing its market value like a leaking tap wastes water. Unnoticed it can continue insidiously until one day, unexpectedly, the tank is empty. She gathered up her notes and hurried from the room, careful to lock up behind her. She must share this success with her boss.

Miss Penney's office was empty. Sally poked her head around the door which stood ajar, but there was no sign of the older woman. It was unusual for Miss Penney to leave her door open, so Sally assumed her boss had simply popped out for a second. She decided to wait and stepped farther into the large, pleasant room.

As she crossed to the desk to lay down her papers, her attention was caught by a scale model on a side table. She walked over and looked at it with fascination. It was perfect. There were the small houses, roads marked, one or two tiny cars in a park and even trees and hedges. She smiled, thinking how Lucy would love to play with it. She looked closer. Surely that was the Hall? Yes, and there was the drive, passing the Lodge, through the gates, so beautifully made. On it went to the village. Sally could even see her own house, but behind that, there was something wrong. A frown puckered her brows. Where did all those houses come from? There was a card fixed to the corner of the huge board on which the model lay. Little Mithering Hall Development, it said. Sally felt the blood drain from her face. Those houses were in the Home Park.

'Sally? Hello. Were you looking for me?' Sally swung round as Miss Penney entered the room. 'Why whatever is the matter, my dear. You look as if you've seen a ghost.'

'Miss Penny . . . this model . . . it is the Hall Estate, isn't it?'

'Yes. They've done a lovely job. Br . . . brilliant even. The Chairman will be pleased. But what's the problem?'

'Here. These houses. They're in the Home Park.'

'That's right. Aren't they beautiful? I'd like to live in one myself. They're a sort of single storey ranch-type cottage, if that makes sense. Very carefully designed to blend in with their surroundings.'

'But there's no room,' burst out Sally. 'There's no space for houses among the trees of the Park.'

'Not at the moment, no. Chosen trees will be felled, about two thirds or even three-quarters, depending on which density we go for. But the remaining ones will make a fantastic setting for the holiday cottages.'

Sally was aghast. 'You're going to chop down Home Park to make a Holiday Camp? But you can't! That's vandalism. Some of those trees are hundreds of years old.'

It was Miss Penney's turn to be taken aback.

'Of course you won't want to see any of the trees go. I can understand that as you have grown up here. But I assure you there is going to be no holiday camp at the Hall. This is an exclusive development, done in the best of taste. See,' she took off the top of what appeared to be an L-shaped barn. 'Here is the indoor swimming pool with the exercise area and beauty spa next door. The golf course will be over here on the old Home Farm grounds and the small lake here will be enlarged and deepened. We'll fill it with fish for the anglers and those who wish can also row over to have picnics on this island we shall create. I assure you Sally it will all be beautiful.'

'And what about the village?'

'Of course the scheme will provide work for local people for many years to come.'

Sally could see she was fighting a losing battle. She shook her head. 'It won't be the same,' she muttered.

Miss Penney smiled. 'Probably not, but that's progress. Now what did you want to see me about?'

As Sally walked home that evening she fought against the tears which had threatened all day. She had spent most of her waking hours for the last few weeks immersed in company books trying to find what was wrong. At last she had succeeded. But gone was the pleasure she had felt that morning. Miss Penney had been delighted and full of praise for Sally's competence. She had even been promised a hefty bonus, but all satisfaction of a job well done was overshadowed by her discovery of the plans for Little Mithering.

That night, once the children were in bed, she told Bob Fletcher what she had learned. He shook his head.

'That's bad, Sally girl, very bad. It's a crying shame to cut those trees. There's none of them diseased. No good reason to bring them down.'

'None but money,' said Sally bitterly. 'And the village, Dad. Just think of it. Everyone'll be up in arms when they find out.'

But Bob wasn't so sure. 'Hang on a minute, girl. There's some folk would welcome a bit of life and change about the place. Fred Tucker, at the pub, wouldn't say no to more custom. And then there's Mrs Wilson. I suppose these holiday people will read newspapers and need supplies?'

'Don't be too sure, Dad. I saw one building labelled 'restaurant' and another 'retail facilities', surely that means shops and somewhere to eat and drink? Far from promoting business in the village, it could be the death of it. What if the people who work there get discounts at the shops on site? They're not going to turn it down to keep Mrs Wilson in business, are they? Oh, I wish Brad was here. He'd know what to do.'

'I did read somewhere that a village got a preservation order on an old tree,' offered Bob.

'I know. I thought of that. But a whole park? And one that is privately owned by the very people who want to destroy it? I hate Lindsey Enterprises.' Sally exclaimed and banged the iron down hard on the inoffensive shirt she was ironing. 'I wish they'd never come here.'

She made the same passionate statement to Chris the next evening. He had persuaded her to come out for a drink at the local pub. Bob Fletcher was only too glad to encourage the outing. Anything to get Sally out of the house and give Bob's ears a bit of peace.

Chris had listened with an expressionless face to Sally's revelations about the proposed development. In answer to her plea for help to save the trees, he became thoughtful.

'When does the work start?'

'I don't know. I didn't think to ask Miss Penney. Now she knows how much I hate the whole thing she may not tell me. But I could ask. I just wish horrid Lindsey Enterprises had never come here.'

Chris looked at her indignant face, opened his mouth to speak, then closed it again. He let Sally finish her drink and got her a refill before he broached the subject again.

'I would say your best bet to get anything changed would be a direct request to the boss.'

'I've told you, she thinks it's great.'

'No. Not F . . . for a minute. I mean the big boss. The person she is answerable to. What's his name?' He hung on Sally's reply as if it was terribly important.

'I don't know. He's never been down here. I suppose it would be the Chairman of Lindsey Enterprises. She's mentioned him once or twice. But I've never met him. Do you really think it would do any good to approach him personally?'

Chris hid a smile. 'I think that is probably the only way anything could ever be changed at this stage,' he answered. 'You go for it Sally. I shall watch with interest to see if you succeed.'

'Alright. I will. I'll ask Miss Penney when the big man is coming down and then ask for an interview. I've just done some good work for him so he should be pleased with me.' Wrapped up as she was with the problems of the Hall Estate, Sally nearly let slip details of her work.

'What's that then?' Chris wanted to know.

'Oh, nothing exciting. Just boring old figures,' Sally hastened to cover her mistake. 'But when the sums add up it helps to keep the clients happy.'

Chapter Twelve

Sally arrived in good time for work next day. She was determined to convince Miss Penney she should be granted an interview with the unknown Chairman of Lindsey Enterprises. But she was out of luck. Miss Penney was nowhere to be found.

'Gorn off up to Town, ducky,' the friendly housekeeper told her. 'Maybe a few days, she ses to me. We're to just carry on as normal wivout 'er.'

Sally was deeply disappointed. All night she had been rehearsing what she would say to persuade Miss Penney, who no doubt thought the development was none of Sally's business and she shouldn't interfere. Now she had to wait for heaven knew how long before she could even make the appointment. If only the builders, or worse still, the tree fellers didn't arrive before Miss Penney was back.

Sally spent that day and the next trying to keep her mind off her two big worries, but whenever she pulled her thoughts away from Brad, they turned to the Home Park. Trying not to fret uselessly about that, her thoughts went back to Brad. Even her work didn't help. Now her special project was finished, the mundane daily entries in the Hall books she could take care of in her sleep.

It was the same over the weekend. She moved about her usual tasks in a dream, not hearing when she was spoken to and losing the thread of any conversation she tried to follow. Chris arrived for Sunday lunch and, seeing the state Sally was in, tried to distract her. His lively nonsense kept the children in fits of laughter. Even Bob chuckled and shook his head, but Sally simply gave a sweet smile and carried on with her domestic tasks. After lunch, in desperation, Chris dragged her and the children into Home Park to play Hide, Go Seek and Catch, their own noisy version of two favourite games. Lucy and Philip thoroughly enjoyed themselves as they dodged, shrieking, between the trees to evade capture. But when Chris found Sally, she had her arms stretched as far around a huge oak tree as she could reach them. Her cheek was pressed to the bark and tears streamed down her face. Chris cursed himself for his insensitivity.

'I'm sorry Sally. I'm such a fool. I didn't think.'

'It's not your fault,' Sally sobbed. 'I'm being such an idiot. Look at me. Crying for a tree. But I'm not really. It's just everything. Oh, I wish Brad was here.' Her tears fell faster. 'When will he come home, Chris? It's been so long. I try to be brave and strong, but I miss him so much. You do think he's alright, don't you?'

Chris hesitated before he answered. A move which Sally noticed.

'Chris. What's the matter? Do you know something I don't?' Sally's tears were dried in an instant. She rubbed her wet eyes with the back of her hand. 'Tell me. What is it?'

'It's nothing concrete. I just heard a rumour from a mutual friend that something is going down in London in which I thought Brad would be involved.'

'What are you talking about? Have you heard from Brad?'

'No. But I'm sure whatever is happening now is as a result of his travels. So, hopefully, he could be coming home soon.'

Sally shook her head. 'I hate it when people talk in riddles. But I suppose it's no use trying to get you to be more specific. But you do think Brad's alright?'

'I think we'd have heard if he wasn't,' Chris answered cautiously and with that Sally had to be content.

On Monday morning Miss Penney had returned. There was almost an air of excitement about her when Sally was called in to the big office.

'Well done, Sally.'

Sally's eyebrows rose in surprise. 'What have I done?'

'Provided the final piece of a jigsaw puzzle which has enabled the police to move in on a particularly nasty customer. Raids were carried out very early this morning and several people were arrested. Br . . . brilliant work, my dear. The Chairman will be delighted.'

'Ah! The Chairman. Can I see him? Can I make an appointment?'

'I'm afraid that's not possible at the moment.'

'But why? You said he'd be pleased with my work. Doesn't that count for anything?'

'Of course it does. That's not the point. I'm afraid he's abroad at the moment.'

'Oh! Well, when's he coming back? I really would like to see him as soon as possible.'

Did she see a shadow cross the older woman's face?

'I don't know, Sally. I'm not sure when he'll be back, but I will, of course, keep you informed of any developments.'

With that Sally had to be content. She brought Miss Penny up to date with what had happened in her absence and frittered away the rest of the day in rebellious mood. She felt so helpless. No Brad, and now no way to try and stop the destruction of the ancient trees.

Next morning Sally dragged herself into work, fed up with her job, Lindsey Enterprises and everything to do with them. On her desk was a note from Miss Penney. 'See me'. Sally looked at it with a sour expression. Now what? More detective work? That would be better than the day to day running of the house, but she couldn't work up any enthusiasm. She left her office and walked slowly up the wide hallway.

Before she reached Miss Penney's room, the door was flung open and Sally's boss shot out in front of her. The older woman's eyes shone. She smiled brilliantly as she looked over Sally's shoulder. Instinctively Sally turned her head and immediately forgot Miss Penney, Lindsey Enterprises and why she stood in the hall. Her heart jumped into the back of her throat where it beat frantically. Her mouth opened but she couldn't breathe or speak. For long moments she froze where she stood, then the spell was broken.

'Brad! Oh, Brad!' she cried as she sped down the long hallway and threw herself into his arms. He staggered as she launched herself into his embrace.

'Sally? Sally? What's going on? What are you doing here? Oh, my darling girl, my little love.'

After his first incredulous exclamations, Brad's reaction to Sally's presence in his arms was all she could have wished. He wrapped himself around her and held her so tightly she could have sworn she heard a rib crack, but she was beyond caring. It was only when she felt her head swim, not from desire but lack of oxygen, that she pummelled his back with her fists, fighting to be free. Reluctantly he loosed his hold on her.

'What's wrong? Sally, what is it?' He frowned down at her. The unruly lock of hair fell over his forehead and his eyes were almost black with hunger for this woman he loved so deeply.

'I just need to breathe occasionally,' Sally wheezed, gasping the air into her lungs. 'It's an annoying habit I have. Sorry.' The imp of teasing mischief was in her eyes. She saw Brad's lower lip tremble and paused. What had she said? She couldn't know how he had longed for that sight as he lay feverish and helpless so far away from her.

'My Sally. OK. I'll let you breathe, but not here. Let's go to the lodge.'

Sally looked back to where Miss Penny stood surveying the unusual scene with remarkable calm. 'I suppose you'd like the rest of the day off, Sally?' Her voice was serious, but a smile tugged at the corners of her mouth.

'Yes, please,' Sally smiled back, her heart so full of love and thankfulness that Brad was safe, she could have kissed her boss for being so understanding. 'There's nothing urgent really, is there? Nothing that can't wait till tomorrow?'

Miss Penney laughed. 'No. Off you go. No doubt I'll hear all about it later,' she finished significantly and went back into her office.

Slowly Sally floated back to earth. She could feel herself smiling idiotically, but somehow she just couldn't stop. It didn't matter. She felt wonderful. Warm, and soft, and fulfilled.

She barely remembered how they had reached the lodge. As soon as they were inside, Brad had swept her into his arms and kicked the door shut behind them. Then he held her away from him and simply looked at her, staring at her from her toes to her hair with an intensity that almost burned her. His grasp on her upper arms was so strong the fingers dug into her flesh, but Sally welcomed the pain. It made this whole scene real. Brad was actually here. This wasn't one of her delicious daydreams but Brad in the flesh, here in the lodge. She looked back at him with her heart in her eyes.

'It's you,' Brad muttered. 'It's really you.'

Sally smiled. She knew what he was saying. He spoke her thoughts. 'Hello, you,' she said softly, in her eyes the teasing look he loved so much 'What kept you?'

Brad moved his hands from her arms to her head, threading his fingers through her hair to hold her face up to his gaze. There he found the welcome he had dreamed of. Keeping his eyes on hers, he slowly lowered his head until his breath feathered across her mouth. Sally's last conscious thought had been a longing for his kiss. Then his lips claimed hers and she was lost in sensation.

With a muffled groan Brad had enfolded her in his arms, his kiss so deep it demanded her complete surrender. Like bolts of lightning desire shot through Sally until every nerve ending quivered in response to Brad's touch. She was on fire, boneless, yielding her feminine softness into his hard male dominance. Lips moved on lips, tongues met and danced together, hands caressed, roving over his strong muscular back and her sleek lines and feminine curves. They couldn't get enough of each other. Touching, holding, kissing, they moved into the bedroom and fell entwined across the coverlet of the double bed. Impatient to get even closer they tore at buttons and helped each other with clinging cloth.

Sally's mouth was swollen with Brad's kisses, her eyes glazed with passion. He had stroked, nibbled, kissed and caressed every inch of her body, brought her to ecstasy, her cries lost against his mouth. She was radiant, aglow with love and satisfaction, but deep within her lazy consciousness a thought niggled. Brad had brought her to the edge of passion and tipped her over into spiralling whirls of amazing sensation, but alone. Didn't he know how much she loved him? This was her man, her love. She wanted to give him everything. To be his totally. He loved her, she knew that. During their passionate embraces he had called her name so often, declared his unending love, but then why had he not made her his completely? Sally turned her passion-glazed eyes to Brad. He was lying beside her, propped up on his elbow, his head resting on his hand, watching her with an expression on his face that made Sally catch her breath. Deep in her belly curls of desire rose again. Did this man know what he did to her? She put out her hand and stroked his chest, her fingers spread out over his well-defined muscles. She could feel his heart beat and smiled in satisfaction as she saw him stiffen and catch his breath. She revelled in her power to arouse him, then frowned. She did arouse him. She knew that. He wanted her, no doubt as fiercely as she desired him, then why? Her hand moved down his chest, over the dip of his waist to the swell of his hip. There it met material. With shocked eyes open wide Sally looked down to Brad's navy Y-fronts, then up to his face. His eyes were rueful.

'Brad, why?' Sally couldn't say more. This wasn't false modesty. They were both long past that stage . . . and so quickly. She chuckled for a moment. Here she was almost naked, relaxed under the gaze of Brad's loving eyes, and he still had his underpants on. She didn't understand. 'I know you want me, and you must know I want to be yours, totally, so why?'

'Of course I want you. If you only knew how hard it's been for me not to let go. Hence the underpants to help my good intentions. You'll probably kill me for this, but I'm sorry, darling, I haven't got any protection. I was in such a hurry to get home to you I didn't do any shopping. And I was lucky enough to hop on and off planes with barely time to spare. So I have nothing with me. Unless you're on the pill?' he finished hopefully.

Sally shook her head. There'd been no man in her life since Brian. It had seemed stupid to go on taking medication she didn't need. But to think Brad, surely a man of the world, didn't have a condom. And here they were together at last, where they had both longed to be. No condom. The thought amazed her, then she saw the funny side and started to chuckle. Soon Brad joined in and the pair of them chortled until their sides ached.

Tears ran down Sally's cheeks as she giggled. Then suddenly they were no longer tears of laughter but real tears, interspersed with heart-wrenching sobs. At last she could let go the iron discipline she had held over her fears for so long. Brad was back and all her horrid imaginings could be banished.

He took her in his arms and rocked her, soothing and petting. He let her go, just long enough to pull the big cover off the bed to wrap around them both, then he let her cry away her fears.

At last her tears ran out. She snuffled and sniffed and finally blew her nose in the large white handkerchief Brad held out to her.

'Sorry, but I think I probably needed that.'

Brad smiled and kissed the top of her head. 'Poor Sally. It's been hard for you, my darling, hasn't it? Believe me if I could have made contact, I would have done. But surely Chris told you the cards meant I was safe?'

'I didn't tell Chris.'

'What? Why not? Surely I told you, you could trust him?'

'Yes. But that was when you first went away. Presumably you didn't know what was going to happen then?'

Brad started to laugh. 'So Chris has no idea I've made contact?'

'No. I interpreted your first card to mean whatever you were doing was serious and I had to tell no-one. I imagined if you'd wanted Chris to know you'd have told him, sent him a card too or something.'

Brad shook his head, still chuckling. 'My clever, honest, trustworthy Sally. What a good special agent you would make.'

Sally was piqued. Brad was laughing at her. Didn't he realise how awful it had been for her? All alone, not being able to tell anyone her fears. She pulled a face at Brad, frowning and sticking out her lower lip in a menacing scowl.

'Oops! Sorry, my love. I'm not laughing at you. I think you've been brilliant. You almost literally held my life in your hands. It couldn't have been in a safer place.'

At his words Sally's eyes grew round as saucers. Was he joking? 'Brad you're frightening me. Now you're safely home can you tell me what happened?'

'Yes. Now I can, and you deserve no less than the whole story. Shall we get right into the bed and make ourselves comfortable? It's going to take a while. Would you like a cup of tea?'

At the mention of tea Sally suddenly thought of the time. How long had they been at the lodge? When had Brad arrived back? Was he hungry?

Brad laughed again at Sally's questions. 'My   poor darling. Back in Sally-the-carer mode, are you? I am a bit hungry actually. I can never enjoy meals on planes, and I came here straight from the airport. Perhaps it would be a good idea to get dressed now. While I eat I can tell you about my adventures.' With one kiss on Sally's forehead, 'that's the only place I can trust myself to kiss you just now,' Brad swung out of bed and started to put on his trousers.

Sally followed his lead reluctantly. She looked around for her clothes which seemed to be scattered in a trail from the living room to the bedside. 'Have you seen Dad? Did he tell you where I was?'

'No. What *were* you doing up at the Hall?'

'I work there.'

'You what?'

'I work there as a book-keeper, an accountant. And that reminds me Brad,' she spoke as she moved into the kitchen to begin preparing some food for him, so she missed his horrified expression. 'There's something I need your help with. You'll never guess what's been going on while you've been away.'

Brad walked into the kitchen tying his tie. 'What's that then?'

At that moment the telephone rang. With a quick glance at Sally, Brad shrugged and went to answer it, pulling the door closed behind him. Sally pulled a loaf out of the deep-freeze and broke off four slices. While these were softening in the microwave, she inspected the cupboards. Chris must eat out a lot. There wasn't much to choose from, but she did find eggs in the fridge. By the time Brad returned, she had cooked him scrambled eggs on toast and had more toast to offer with honey or jam. The coffee was nearly ready as he came through the door.

'That smells wonderful. I hadn't realised how hungry I was,' his eyebrows rose suggestively as he leered at Sally. 'You take my mind off things, Miss Fletcher,' he growled.

Sally laughed and blushed. Now, standing in the kitchen, fully dressed, the memory of the love they had shared, the things they had done to each other sent a wave of longing through her. Quickly she sat down at the table before her knees gave way and betrayed her.

Brad reached across and took her hand. He raised it to his lips and kissed each knuckle. 'That's just a beginning, my darling,' he promised. 'I confess I forgot Chris might walk in on us. Next time, I'll make sure there'll be no interruptions.'

Sally caught her lip between her teeth. Chris. She'd forgotten all about him. The imp of mischief was back in her eyes. 'Thank goodness we got away with it. But, at least it would have shown I was telling the truth,' she finished with a put-on air of innocence.

'What are you talking about?'

'What's all this about you pinching each other's girlfriends?'

Brad frowned, then looked confused and finally gave a short laugh and a shake of his head. 'The devil. What's he been telling you?'

'Never mind what he's been telling me. I want to know what's been happening to you.'

'I'm sorry, darling. That'll have to wait. That phone-call was from the police in London. I have to go. I'll explain everything, and I do mean everything when I get back. Please be patient a little longer?'

Sally felt a thrill of panic rush through her. 'Brad. Please don't go? Please? Stay with me. Or let me come with you?'

He took her in his arms. 'Darling. I wish I could, but Jim's outside now, waiting. The sooner I go, the sooner I'll be back. I love you so much. Surely you know I'm never going to let you go again?'

He kissed her once, hard and long, then he was gone.

Sally tidied up the little kitchen, then thought of Chris's return and hurried into the bedroom to smooth the rumpled bed. As she let herself out of the lodge she smiled at the thought of Chris's face when he learned she had kept secrets from him. But she hadn't meant to. Or anyway she'd only done it for Brad's sake. She hated secrets and lies.

As she walked along the road towards the cottage Sally wondered how Brad had found her at the Hall. If he hadn't seen Bob, then who had told him where to find her? But, hang on, he hadn't expected her to be there had he? He had been surprised to find her there. What was going on?

Chapter Thirteen

Sally's shining eyes told their own story when Bob came home that night. He smiled and hugged his eldest child with a thankful heart. At last things seemed to be going right for her. She had given up so much for the sake of him and the children, she deserved her chance of happiness. He wouldn't stand in her way. If she and Brad were to marry, Bob would manage somehow.

'So where is he then? I'd have thought you'd not let him out of your sight.'

He frowned and shook his head when he heard of Brad's appointment with the police. He frowned even harder when he realised Sally still didn't know where Brad had been for so long.

'Although it must have been somewhere hot,' she offered. 'He was as brown as a berry, but thinner, much thinner,' she remembered. Heat or illness? Or lack of food? She pushed the thought away. Whatever it had been he was safe back home now and soon he would tell her all about his adventures.

A very satisfactory, long telephone call that evening brought a blush to her cheeks and a tender smile to her lips as Bob tried not to overhear her words. At last he stepped out into the garden to give the lovebirds some privacy. If he were young Brad he'd want his girl to return some of the sweet nothings she was obviously hearing. It would be good to have Brad back. Bob had missed their talks. Tied as he was with a young family he rarely joined the regulars in the pub. It had been a pleasant change to have another man about the house.

Sally went to sleep that night with her bedroom curtains open wide. She blew a kiss to the moon, hoping that Brad, as promised, was looking up at it too. He had to attend at least two identity parades he had said, and make a long statement, so it was unlikely he would be home tomorrow. But the day after would be theirs.

She hadn't asked him how he knew she was at the Hall, or rather, why he was there when he didn't know she would be there too. All that could wait till they were together again. With his arms around her she would nestle her head into that perfect fit, just below his collarbone, and he could tell her all about his travels. He would explain everything satisfactorily, she was sure. With a happy smile on her lips, Sally fell asleep.

Next morning Sally flew through the side door of the Hall, threw her coat at a peg in the small cloakroom and hurriedly slid onto the chair behind her desk. The clock pointed accusingly at ten past nine. For the very first time, Sally was late. She had been all fingers and thumbs this morning and the children had been exasperating. Once they knew Brad was back, they asked countless questions, demanding answers Sally couldn't give. She couldn't be cross with them, her heart was singing with joy. So there was laughter and teasing and promises to tell all as soon as she knew. The time rushed past and the usually efficient Sally found her thoughts straying from the tasks in hand. So here she was, late.

She booted up her computer and turned to the paperwork on her desk. But she was up to date with everything. Sally thought for a moment. She could spend the morning idling away her time, gazing into space and thinking of Brad. That would be her preferred option. But she was too honest to think of that for long. Besides with work to occupy her mind, the time would pass more quickly until Brad's arrival. So she got up to find Miss Penney and whatever task needed attention.

As she reached her boss's office and raised her hand to knock, Sally heard her name. The door in front of her wasn't properly closed and the unseen speaker's voice came clearly to Sally's ears.

'Thank God you didn't tell Sally anything, Farthing. Brad would have been furious.'

That was Chris's voice. Sally frowned. What was he doing here in Miss Penney's office? And who was he talking to? Farthing? That was Brad's personal assistant, wasn't it? The woman who had spoken to Sally on the telephone in the lodge. What was she doing here? The questions raced through her mind.

'I could kill Brad.' That was Miss Penney's voice. 'First he disappears for weeks on end without a word, and then once he's back I have to rely on a telephone call from London to explain everything. It's too bad. And it's not my fault Sally's working here. How was I to know she was in the dark?'

'The way I did, duckie, by catching on PDQ. The number of times I nearly spilt the beans on our first meeting. Talk about skating on thin ice. But what did he say to you yesterday about Sally?'

'He said we're to keep our mouths shut. That's all.'

'You mean he doesn't want her to know the truth? But surely . . .?'

'Don't ask me. I only work here.' Miss Penney's voice was sharp, indignant even, as though she wasn't used to being kept in the dark and resented it now.

Silently Sally stepped away from the door and hurried back to her own office. She was shaken and needed solitude to sort out her whirling thoughts.

Miss Penney was Farthing. That seemed clear. Of course! Penny farthing. Sally groaned. Could it be that silly, or that simple? Assuming it was true, Farthing was Brad's right-hand man, or rather woman. Chris was Brad's best, maybe only, friend. So it was plain they would know each other. Then why keep it a secret? And why hadn't Brad told her Farthing was at Little Mithering? What was his connection with Lindsey Enterprises? Did he work for them too? A roving commission perhaps, like the one he had for his old patron, Jock? Or did Miss Penney have two jobs? Sally shook her head. Nothing made sense.

She looked out of the window, her unfocused eyes not registering the beauty of the sunny day which turned the autumn leaves to a glory of vibrant colour. She tried to think logically about what had happened.

Brad had come to the lodge because Farthing had fixed everything up after his accident. Had she persuaded her employers to rent out the lodge to Brad? The estate had been sold before he arrived. And he knew that. He'd spoken of changes on their first meeting.

A distant movement caught her attention. From her window Sally saw Chris's back view. He was walking rapidly as he came into view, then followed the curve of the drive out of sight again. A tap on her door made Sally jump. Miss Penney walked in.

'Sally I'd like you to . . . whatever is the matter, my dear? You look dreadfully pale. Are you alright?'

Sally shook her head and tried to gather her scattered wits. 'I . . . er . . . I do feel a bit peculiar,' she managed to mumble. Which was nothing more than the truth. She felt as though the earth had tilted beneath her feet. Everything she trusted, everything she thought she knew about her beloved Brad was not as it seemed.

'Why don't you run along home, then? There's nothing urgent here and you certainly deserve some time off after your heroic stint as Sherlock Holmes.'

Sally watched Miss Penney nod and smile as if from a great distance. What was behind the concern the older woman expressed? Did she want to get rid of Sally in case Brad slipped back to the Hall without notice? He'd come straight here on his arrival home last time, hadn't he? He hadn't gone to the cottage seeking Sally, the woman he said he loved and would never leave. Sweet words. But were they true?

Like an automaton Sally switched off her computer, gathered up her belongings and walked home. Sally remembered thankfully that Dad was not due home for lunch today. For a few hours she would have the cottage to herself. Precious hours of solitude when she could think, uninterrupted by demands on her time and attention. She made herself coffee and sat at the kitchen table, hands wrapped around the mug, not drinking, but grateful for the comforting warmth. She tried to marshal her thoughts into rational facts.

Fact one was that she loved Brad. Two was that he loved her in return. Didn't he? Yes, he did. He'd told her both before he went away and after he came back. So if they loved each other, why all this secrecy?

He'd said there was something important he wanted to tell her. She'd thought, and hoped it was that he loved her and wanted to spend the rest of his life with her. But what if he'd meant something else?

Before he'd left for his trip, he'd been worried she might learn something while he was away. Was he thinking of Farthing being Miss Penney? Hardly. He couldn't have known Sally would ever go anywhere near the Hall, so it was hardly likely she would have found that out in his absence. What then?

Sally's worried thoughts skeetered this way and that to find a solution. She thought of Chris's words that morning.

'You mean he doesn't want her to know the truth?' That's what he had said. Brad didn't want Sally to know the truth. About what? And if he didn't want her to know, then he wasn't going to tell her. Was he?

'He said we're to keep our mouths shut.' That's what Miss Penney had said. Brad had ordered that Sally be kept in ignorance of . . . of . . . what?

Sally banged her fist down on the table in frustration, spilling her cold coffee. With an exclamation of exasperation, she jumped up, dumped the rest of the coffee down the drain and wiped the table with short angry movements. Just as she was wringing out the cloth the front doorbell rang. Sally's heart leapt. Brad. She rushed towards the door, then slowed. He had said this evening. Maybe he couldn't wait and had come home early? Or maybe it wasn't Brad at all? She didn't want to see anyone else. Cautiously she moved to the window and peeked through the crack where the curtain met the wall. Chris. No way. Knowing him, he'd come round the back in a minute to see if she was in the garden. Swiftly and silently Sally sped across the kitchen, grabbed her keys and slid out of the back door, locking it behind her. She fled down the garden path and through the gate into Home Park. Her beloved trees would hide her from Chris and his smiling lies. She wanted answers, but not from him.

Chapter Fourteen

Sally crossed the road to wait for the school bus. She had spent hours in Home Park, wandering among the trees. At first it had been simply to stay there long enough for Chris to give up and go away. But then she started remembering all the happy times she had spent there as a child and time ceased to matter.

Her first conscious memory was being underneath the leafy branches of a huge tree. Memory or a tale often told? She thought she remembered the sunshine piercing the leaves in bars of golden light and the squirrel, then Mother had told the tale so often since, perhaps it wasn't a Sally memory at all? But looking back it seemed so real. The sleek, cheeky animal carrying its bushy tail in an arc behind it, stopping to chatter to the child in the pushchair below, then at some trigger of alarm, dropping the acorn from its paw - the acorn which fell into the lap of that little girl.

'Gilla!' she'd cried and pointed up.

Sally smiled. 'Gillas' they had remained during her childhood and even Philip and Lucy called squirrels by Sally's baby name.

There had been picnics she really did remember. Mother had provided delicious food for hearty appetites as Sally and her friends had chased and laughed beneath the trees. There'd been birthday celebrations and walks too, with Dad and Mother, learning the names of flowers and bushes, trees and herbs. And later, in their grief and loneliness, Sally and Bob had found some solace in the company of the ancient trees Mother had loved so much.

Laurence hadn't liked trees, Sally noted with a wry smile. Surely that should have told her something about him? How could anyone not love their beauty and venerable grandeur? Of course, Miss Penney hadn't seemed impressed, she remembered. And there she was, back in the present with all its problems and questions. A glance at her watch told Sally she must hurry if she wanted to meet the children from school and with a last stroke of her hand against the bark of a huge oak, she had reluctantly left her friends.

The children's chatter distracted her, and their needs kept her busy until the hands of the clock had raced around to the time she expected Brad to appear. Sally felt panic fill her chest. She didn't know what to say. She needed more time to think things through, to collect her thoughts and organise her questions. But the clock ticked on and at last the doorbell rang.

Impatient to be with his love, Brad opened the door and called.

'Sally! Bob! Anyone home? Can I come in?'

Bob came forward to greet him with a hearty handshake. 'Glad you're back, lad, safe and well. There's some here have been worrying themselves sick, not knowing what had become of you.' He accompanied the words with a smile, but Brad felt an element of reproof beneath the greeting. Of course Bob didn't know Sally had received word from overseas. Brad smiled at him while he thought how trustworthy Sally had proved. He had put his life in her hands, and she hadn't disappointed him. She hadn't even told Chris. At that thought his smile widened even more. Then he had to cope with two young bodies hurled at him in greeting, as Philip and Lucy demanded to know where he'd been. He bade them go and plunder the carrier bags, which he'd laid down by the door and in the ensuing pandemonium he didn't register Sally's reserve.

He'd always known he couldn't just waltz in and sweep her away from her family, much as he wanted to do just that. But he'd got rid of Chris for the night and as soon as possible he and Sally could go to the lodge and shut the door against the rest of the world. He looked at Bob.

'Any chance of stealing Sally away?'

'I suppose you mean right now?' Bob laughed. 'Go on, you two. I can sort out the kids. Although how I'm ever going to get them calmed down enough for sleep after they've got their hands on all these goodies I don't know. It's like Christmas.'

Brad grinned ruefully. Perhaps he had gone overboard. He'd only meant to get the children one toy each. But once in Hamley's he'd gone a bit mad. He'd never been in a proper toy store before. It called to the boy in him - that little boy who had been grateful to get a colouring book, an annual and a shiny coin at the bottom of a stocking filled with fruit and sweets paid for with his mother's carefully hoarded pennies. He'd enlisted the salesgirl's help for Lucy's gifts and been amazed at how many outfits and accessories had been devised to accompany one Barbie doll to stimulate a small girl's imagination.

'I didn't forget Dad,' he said and rescued a bag from the children. He hoped the autobiography of Bob's favourite footballer would go down well, together with a fleece-lined waistcoat and was rewarded by Bob's speechless face of amazement. 'Come on, Sally,' Brad laughed. 'Before he changes his mind.'

Once safely in the Gate Lodge, with the door closed and bolted, Brad took Sally in his arms.

'I've longed for this moment,' he assured her, gazing into her hazel eyes with a passion he could barely contain. 'When I lay helpless in that forest, you were the only thing that kept me from going out of my mind. I had to get better, to come back to your sweet face and . . .' he pulled her closer and captured her lips in a kiss which said more than words could express. It told her of his need, his love and his hunger for her touch, and a love to match his own. This was what had kept him going, had kept him alive. Sally. His Sally. His love. The woman he had never thought to meet. His soulmate. The only woman who could ever fill that void he carried within him. She could make him whole.

But Sally was struggling to be free. He released her with a laugh.

'Sorry, my darling. I forgot your habit of breathing which tends to interrupt our most interesting moments.' He expected an answering smile from Sally as she remembered the last time she had needed air. But though she was flushed by her response to his kisses, her face was solemn.

'I need to talk to you Brad.'

'And you shall.' His eyes still devoured her, as he hardly dared believe she was really here in his arms. He'd waited so long, deliberately held back from speeding to her side. 'We'll talk for hours. I want to hear all about you. I've got rid of Chris for the night and I've so much to tell you. I never dreamed when we said goodbye it would be for so long. I never intended to leave you like that. You'll hardly believe the things that happened to me. I hardly believe them myself. It sounds more like something out of a boys' adventure story. And to think that all the time it was you . . . '

'Go on, Brad. What was me?'

Damn! He hadn't meant to come to that part yet. It would be better if he could start at the beginning.

'When were you going to tell me that Farthing was Miss Penney?'

Damn, damn and double damn. His mouth closed in a hard line. His nostrils looked pinched. It was a face his employees dreaded to see. Brad's anger was something to be avoided. Normally fair and just, it took a lot to rouse him, but when he felt justifiably annoyed, look out.

'Who the hell has been blabbing about things which don't concern them?'

'Don't concern them? Does that include me?' Sally's red hair was almost vibrating she was so cross. 'How dare you sweep away my questions with talk of other people. This is me. And you are here and you're not going anywhere until I have answers. No-one has been blabbing, as you put it. In fact your loyal friends are still conspiring to keep me thoroughly in the dark. Do you know how stupid that makes me feel? How betrayed? You say you trust me with your life, and I certainly did what you asked, but you couldn't trust me with a few simple facts, like who is who? Would it endanger the safety of the country perhaps? Cause a Third World War?'

Sally had jumped to her feet and was pacing the floor. Her sarcasm was strange to Brad. He opened his eyes wide and listened carefully to her impassioned speech. She was now so angry he could see her shaking. Tears stood in her eyes. He had hurt her and how on earth was he ever going to explain? How could he take away the pain she felt? She thought he had betrayed her - shut her out of parts of his life. Well that was true wasn't it? But no more.

'Sally. Forgive me. Please.' He waited, relying on her essential fairness.

She stopped her pacing and looked out of the window, then turned to face him. 'Why?'

'Various reasons at different times.' He didn't pretend to misunderstand her question. She wanted to know why he hadn't been honest with her. 'If you'll let me, I'll try and tell you why.'

Sally stood where she was and looked at him. Brad held his breath. He tried to put into his beseeching eyes his need for her to give him a chance. At last she sat down on an armchair, away from the couch where they had held each other so intimately on a happier occasion. It seemed like a hundred years ago. Brad let out his breath in a long sigh.

'Please be patient, because I want to tell you the whole story, and for that we have to go back a few years. Please, Sally, let me tell you all of it,' he begged as she opened her mouth, no doubt to ask for a simple explanation. 'Nothing is simple in this life it seems to me. And this story is more complicated than most, so I need to set the scene for you.'

Sally said nothing, but settled more comfortably in her chair, which Brad took to be a sign to proceed.

'I told you about Jock and how he rescued my mother and me from a life of near poverty. He was a just and fair man, but he couldn't stand to be surrounded by bleeding hearts, so I learnt very early on to keep any doubts and fears from him. I kept my mouth shut but my ears open. I kept my own counsel and got on all right. People may think I'm hard and heartless.' His lips twisted as he remembered that phrase hurled at him in the past by two women who would have liked to become Mrs Picton. 'I've had to be to survive.'

Sally's face was expressionless. Did she think he was looking for sympathy?

'When Jock died, I was very comfortably off financially, but I lost the only true friend I'd ever had, apart from Chris and he's different. Jock was my guide and mentor, the real father I never had. He left me nothing in his will and that was fine. I expected to have nothing more to do with the Masterson family.' He saw Sally frown and sit up at that point. What had he said of special interest? Why couldn't he put this better? He should be used to presenting cases to persuade people to his way of thinking. He'd done it often enough in the Boardroom. But persuading Sally he was trustworthy was much more difficult and important. His whole happiness rested on his success. Brad ploughed on.

'Some of my money I had invested in Jock's companies. After his death, Adrian took over and disaster wasn't far behind. His mother had kept him away from Jock, so he knew very little about the business. Jock had appointed key people to help and advise his son but, unfortunately, he had left overall power in Adrian's hands. The son soon got rid of his father's best people and proceeded to make one mistake after the other, always with an eye to generating ready money without safeguards for the future. Three companies of the little empire Jock left his son had gone to the wall, or been broken up to make a fast buck, before I realised what was happening. But then he started undermining one of the firms in which I had quite a large number of shares. I saw the danger and challenged him on his course of action.'

Brad stopped and looked away from Sally, away out of the window into the past. The hate and venom in Adrian's eyes had shaken him. The younger man had rejected all offers of help to turn the company round. He had ranted at Brad, screamed out his defiance and a whole load of nonsense about Brad trying to rob him of his heritage. Brad had pointed out, reasonably enough, that Jock had left him nothing in the Will. But somehow such poison had dripped into Adrian's mind, he was beyond reason on the subject of Brad and Jock. He was convinced Brad intended to rob him. Brad shook his head. It had been a very unpleasant scene.

'So what happened next?'

Sally's quiet question brought Brad back to the present with a start.

'He didn't want to know. He seemed to think I was trying to feather my own nest. So I had to work behind the scenes. As the company looked shakier, people got worried. I bought shares at every opportunity and blocked his more extravagant moves with my voting rights as a stockholder. Eventually I gained control of the whole company when Adrian sold a block of his own shares to raise cash.'

'Why did he need money? I thought his father was wealthy?'

'He was and Adrian inherited the lot. But unhappily he has expensive tastes in fast cars which he manages to crash, and an even more expensive drug habit. It just amazes me that neither of them has killed him before this.' He couldn't help the cynical remark. He was so tired of the havoc Adrian had wrought in his life. But no more.

'So you saved the company?'

'Yes. That one and several others. Finally, by last year I had acquired the controlling interest in all but one of Jock's original holdings. I felt I owed it to the old man. He took such pride in his achievement, in his ability to

145

leave his son such an inheritance. It would have broken his heart to see it destroyed.'

A small smile touched Sally's lips.

'What is it? Why are you smiling?'

'I've just seen the warm side of this hard ruthless man you've been telling me about. You really loved Jock, and I've seen that warmer side of you with the children too. You're a fraud Bradney Picton. You're not heartless at all.'

Sally's smile widened. It would be so easy to take her in his arms and show her just how much love he had to give, a love of which he had never thought himself capable. But that must wait. This was his one chance to make a clean breast of everything. Sally had felt shut out. Well, he wasn't going to let her feel that, ever again. She must know the truth, the whole truth, if they were going to be able to move on.

'Caring for anyone makes you vulnerable. I thought I knew that. When my mother died, it was painful. I felt guilty she had suffered so much, even though I had been able to make her life better for the final few years. After she'd gone, there was just Jock, and he could take care of himself. I didn't let myself get close to anyone else. Better alone, than be responsible for someone else's life and happiness.' He had learned in the forest just how vulnerable love could make him. His need for Sally had frightened him by its strength, the other side of which was his own weakness where she was concerned. But even greater than his love had been his fear for her safety, if Adrian had realised Brad was alive and cared for Sally.

'By this time, it really had become a battle between Adrian and me for control of Jock's empire. Adrian used some dirty tricks and tried everything he knew to prevent me acquiring legitimate control. He even sold his own shares at far less than their worth to people who, in return, only had to promise they wouldn't sell them on to me. But he was driven by the need for ready money, and I was prepared to outbid him every time.' His jaw clenched as he thought what it had cost him to get rid of Adrian. 'He never seemed to learn. I really think his obsession turned his brain, that or the drugs, or both.'

'You mean he went mad?'

'Not as you mean, no. I'm afraid he didn't have that excuse. He needed to be sane to plot the devious course which nearly brought about my death.'

Sally's eyes widened at his words. He didn't want to scare her, but he must make her realise.

'The first time Adrian tried to kill me was with the block and tackle on the rig. The blow I received was no accident. Chris went out there and eventually got to the bottom of it. The man who engineered it was new to the job, so able to claim it was an accident, but Chris is like a bulldog. He won't let go until he's got what he wants. There was nothing we could take to court, but we did trace money in the guy's account back to Adrian.' Brad grinned. 'Farthing's a bit of a bulldog too, when it comes to figures.'

Sally had been leaning forward, totally absorbed in Brad's story but, at mention of Farthing's name, she stiffened and sat back in her chair, putting more distance between them. Brad bit his lip and decided to carry on with the whole story instead of cutting to Sally's more recent grievances.

'You know I came here to recuperate. If it hadn't been for you, I'd have gone mad with the enforced inactivity. But, when I was fit again, Chris brought me the news I had been waiting for. I could go and get hold of the final proof which would put Adrian behind bars for fraud at least.

There he could get help to shake off his drug problem, which was what Jock would have wanted.' Brad shook his head in wonder at his own naivety.

'You'd have thought I'd have more sense, wouldn't you? Been more careful? But I went blundering into a very neat trap. I followed the trail which would uncover the fraud and ran into another which led to drug-running. Before I could do anything about it, I was bopped on the head, thrown into a canoe and set adrift on a river in Argentina, or it may have been Paraguay. I think I crossed and recrossed the border several times in the depths of the forest. I was found and rescued by some native villagers. They dosed me with their own brand of medicine to cure me of a nasty attack of malaria. When I was finally strong enough to move, they contacted a German biologist downstream who got me back to civilisation.'

Sally's eyes had grown even rounder as she listened to Brad's tale. As he'd said, it sounded like an adventure story in a comic book. But his face was too serious for make-believe. 'Was that when you sent me the first card in an envelope?'

'Yes. I picked up the card from a colleague and gave the envelope to one of my people in Asuncion. He sent it to Australia where it was posted.'

Sally frowned. 'But there were others afterwards, at intervals. Were they all posted that way?'

'Yes.'

'But why didn't you come home? It was nearly a month after you were rescued, before you came back to England. Wasn't it?' She shook her head in distress. 'I don't even know that do I? You could have been back for ages and I'd never know.' Tears filled her eyes. 'How can I know what's true and what isn't Brad? How could you leave me to worry for so long?'

Brad moved to where she sat in the armchair and hunkered down on his heels in front of her. When he reached out to her, she shrank away, so he put a rein on his need to touch her and went on with his story in a low, urgent voice she had to believe.

'I love you, Sally. After this, I promise you, on everything I hold dear . . .' He cast around in his mind for something which would impress her, make her realise he was telling the truth. 'I promise you on my mother's memory, there'll be no more secrets. You'll know everything and I will answer all your questions, honestly. I didn't dare come home to you for fear Adrian might get to you. He'd tried to kill me twice. If he knew how much you meant to me, he certainly wouldn't hesitate to harm you in order to hurt me. I had to stay dead, as far as he was concerned until he could be stopped. I stayed in hiding but sent out a few trusted people to carry out my orders.' He grinned. 'One advantage of working for Jock all over the world was the network of people I built up, a few casual friends, and many friendly acquaintances, on whom I can call at need. Some are less fussy over legalities than others and they can be very useful. They ask no questions. At last I had every trick in my hands. I came back to London and the police took over. Adrian and his cohorts are all now under lock and key. We have an excellent chance to get him, not only for fraud and drug-running, but attempted murder as well'

Sally hesitated only a few moments. The full horror of Brad's experiences penetrated the wall of resistance she had thrown up against him. Her arms opened as Brad sank to his knees and buried his head in her lap. He looked exhausted. She held him close, stroking her fingers through his hair, feeling the firm shape of his head beneath her palms. His skull had taken cruel blows in his enemy's attempts to kill him. Thank God it was hard and thick enough to protect his life. She smiled. Then a little gurgle of relief escaped her lips.

Brad raised his head to look at her, relieved to see she was smiling. 'What is it, my love?'

'I'm glad you've got a thick head,' she laughed and promptly burst into tears.

Chapter Fifteen

Once Sally's tears had been dried, she hugged and kissed Brad long enough to reassure herself he was quite safe and solid, and still as dear and exciting as ever. But before she got carried away on the tide of passion his lovemaking created, she captured Brad's exploring hands and returned to her questions.

"Behave a bit longer please, Brad. There are still things I don't understand, and they're niggling me. Chris told Miss Penney you didn't want me to know the truth. Why?"

"I didn't want you to find out half the facts, perhaps jumbled and frightening. I wanted to be the one to tell you everything, just as I have now. I was going to tell you all this that evening we should have gone out for dinner. But I was called away, remember? All I could do was to tell you I loved you and ask you trust me in case you did find out something you didn't understand."

"That's all very well, but why the secrecy about Miss Penney. She is your Farthing, isn't she?"

"Yes. It's a pathetically silly nickname I know. I hardly remember how it all came about, it's so long ago. She used to work for Jock. When he died, she came to me. There's no one who knows more about me and my business than Farthing. She's totally trustworthy."

"Unlike me, you mean," said Sally bitterly.

"That's not fair! Farthing has known me for years and years. She's built up my trust through proving herself. But I trust you because I love you. I did trust you, with

151

my life. Even Farthing didn't know I was alive. She heard of my disappearance in the forest and must have had a bad time. She's more than just an employee, we go back so far. But that was all she knew, until I phoned her from the lodge. I only wanted to find out if she was in her office. I didn't give her a chance to tell me you were there too. You came as a delightful surprise." He smiled down at Sally where she lay in the crook of his arm. They shared the softly upholstered depths of the big armchair.

"But you wanted to see her first." Sally's hurt was still raw.

"I wanted to assure her I was alive. I thought I owed her that, after not making contact with anyone here but you. Once I'd got Farthing's worries off my conscience, I could then devote all my time to you. But you were at the Hall."

"Of course. While you were away I got a job there. I'm an accountant. I knew I'd heard that woman's voice somewhere, the very first time I went to the Hall. But I just couldn't place it. It was on the phone that day when you phoned her to send Jim with the car. Miss Penney gave me the job. You must have known I was there. You said earlier, *all the time it was you.* What did that mean?"

"Farthing told me on the phone to London yesterday night that you were the one who had unravelled the book-keeping of the Import/Export company Adrian was using to get his drugs into the country. My clever darling. But that was the first I knew of you working there."

Sally's mouth dropped open. The work she had been doing for Lindsey Enterprises was tied up with Brad's trip and his problems going all the way back to Adrian, Jock's son. Jock!

"What was Jock's name"

"Jock Masterson. Why?"

152

"The old lady who owned the Hall was Mrs Masterson. Any connection?"

"She was Jock's aunt by marriage. He used to talk about this place with more affection than any of the houses Anthea had bought with his money. When Jock was a young man, his uncle started him off in business. He and old Mrs Masterson had no children, so Jock inherited the Hall."

"But you said Jock died five years ago. Mrs Masterson was still alive then."

"Yes, she was, so when she died the Hall went to Adrian. As soon as he put it on the market, I wanted to rescue it. I'm sick of living out of a suitcase, Sally. I had almost decided to make the Hall my home and stop wandering around the world with no ties and no place to lay my head. Then I met you," he smiled down at her upturned face. "All my Christmases came at once. I did try to resist you, particularly when I thought you were so much younger, a teenage Mum. Once that nonsense was sorted out, I thought we could enjoy a pleasant friendship. Then you tugged at my senses, and I assured myself a light flirtation, a holiday romance perhaps, while I recuperated, would do no harm. But I had no defence against you, Sally Fletcher. You invaded my head, my thoughts, my senses and finally my heart, until you had captured all of me.

"I realised just how empty my life was before we met, as I lay weak and helpless in that forest clearing. There was I, big Brad Picton, with more money than I can spend in a lifetime, staff who jump to do my bidding and the power to make or break people in business. I lay in that hammock and all I could think of was you. I didn't need the rest, my trappings of wealth and power. I just longed for one slim laughing girl with sparkling eyes and the cheek to tease and contradict me whenever it took her fancy. Oh! my Sally! It was you and you alone who saved me then." He buried his face in her hair and held her close.

Sally could feel the pounding of his heart. She put her arms as far around his broad back as she could reach and felt him shaking. A wave of love surged through her. She was awed by her power over Brad, as he had revealed it in his anguished tones. He'd said he was wealthy, mega rich by the sound of it, but it meant nothing without the fulfilment her love could bring him. Once before she'd longed to love him so much she would chase away the memories of his loneliness. Now that he had declared his love for her and his great need, Sally's heart swelled with an outpouring of that love. She pulled back from his embrace and took his face between her two palms.

"You don't have to be alone any more, Brad. I'm here. I love you and always will."

She gasped as the breath was crushed out of her lungs by the strength of his arms. But she had seen the look of wonder, of worship, on his face as her words penetrated his mind. He looked like a man who had been saved from the abyss. For a moment she wondered just what horrors he had suffered, not only in the forest, but in the lonely years after his mother died.

Then Brad cradled her in his arms looked down at her.

"Tonight, my darling, you are going to be loved and worshipped, as no other woman has ever been loved before."

A thrill of expectation ran through Sally's body. Goose-bumps sprang up on her skin. She shivered.

He was in no hurry now. Brad had promised her worship, and he was the worshipper. He started at her forehead with a brush of the lips, then Sally was lost in sensation. When he broke off the caresses Sally felt bereft, lost without that contact to the man whose body called to hers with such insistence.

She was beyond thought as she returned his kisses. Brad gathered her closer into his arms, holding her to him until with a groan he loosed his hold. They rested in that drifting state between sleeping and waking. It felt so right to be together.

Sally smiled into Brad's happy eyes and stretched.

"I must go."

"I don't want you to."

"I don't want to either, but I must be there at breakfast time, otherwise there'll be too many questions I don't want to answer . . . yet." She smiled again and slid, reluctantly, out of his arms. "Have another nap and come over after the kids have gone to school."

"You don't think I'm going to let you walk home alone, do you? Where are my trousers?"

Arms around each other, they strolled through the crisp Autumn night. Sally's head rested in the hollow of Brad's shoulder. There was no need for words. They were at peace. An owl hooted from the direction of Home Park and rustles in the hedges indicated small night creatures hurrying about their business. At the door of the cottage Brad gave Sally a gentle kiss.

"'Til tomorrow."

"Later this morning you mean," she whispered. "Come as soon as you can. I hate having to leave you now."

"I'll be here after breakfast, then we'll have to talk and plan. I have no intention of letting you leave me for much longer Sally Fletcher. Sleep well, my love."

Sally got ready for bed with a dreamy smile on her face. She gazed in the mirror as she brushed her hair.

Sally Fletcher. Sally Picton. Mrs Sally Picton. Mr and Mrs Brad Picton.

She fell asleep seeing small boys with Brad's face and little girls with her own chestnut curls playing among the trees in Home Park.

Chapter Sixteen

'Everything alright, girl?' Bob Fletcher rested a hand on Sally's shoulder on his way to take his seat at the breakfast table.

'Fine, Dad, thanks.' Sally threw him a brilliant smile as she deftly flipped over the egg in the frying pan. 'Come on you two. Stop messing about. Lucy, finish your milk. Philip, take those marbles off the table and eat your toast. Here you are, Dad.' She laid Bob's plate in front of him, dried Lucy's milky mouth and then helped the small girl with her shoelaces. 'Are you in for lunch, Dad?'

'No. I'll grab a bite at the pub in Libchester. That job's nearly finished. I wonder when this scheme at the Hall is starting up. If I got some of the work there, it could keep me going for months. And very handy for home.'

'Dad! How could you?'

'Sticking your head in the sand isn't going to change anything, Sally. If the work goes ahead, then I shall put in for it. Better giving work to local folk than bringing in strangers from Libchester and elsewhere.'

'I know that's right. But I'm hoping Brad will help me with a campaign to save the trees. He can walk me to work this morning. We hardly had time to make plans last night.' She blushed a little and smiled as she thought how they had spent their precious time together. 'I'm still hoping to see the Chairman of Lindsey Enterprises when he gets back from abroad. Chris said that would be my best bet.' She stopped as a new thought struck her. 'Brad must know him too, because Brad's the new owner of the

Hall – I think.' What exactly had Brad said? He wanted to rescue the Hall, but that didn't mean he'd bought it, did it? But he had said he wanted to make it his home. Was he going to share it with Lindsey Enterprises or lease it from them? Or perhaps he was hoping to buy one of the houses in the new leisure complex? Oh, no. Surely not?

By the time she had seen the children on to the School Bus and tidied up the kitchen Sally was watching the time with an anxious eye. If Brad didn't come soon, she would be late for work. Just as she decided she could wait no longer, he arrived. She scooped up her keys and bag and hurried to the door to greet him. His good morning kiss was turning into something much warmer and deeper when Sally at last broke free.

'Coming up for air again?' Brad teased, still holding her in the circle of his arms. He looked down at her business suit. 'My! You're looking very smart this morning.'

Sally smiled up at him. 'It's how I usually dress for the office,' she said, wondering if he had even noticed what she had been wearing on Tuesday when he had turned up so unexpectedly at the Hall. He should remember, she thought with a grin, he had taken it off, piece by piece.

'But you're not going to work today.'

'Of course I am. I had most of yesterday off. I can't make a habit of it and I haven't been working there long enough to earn much holiday.'

'No, it's alright. I've squared it with Farthing. She's not expecting you today.'

Sally opened her mouth, then closed it again. If she spoke now, she might say something she'd regret. But how dare Brad do such a thing? He had no business to interfere in her working life. She pressed her lips together while she got her simmering temper under control and looked up at him. He had no idea he'd done anything wrong. He was smiling at her with such uncomplicated happiness, she hadn't the heart to spoil his mood. After all he'd only just got back from a terrible time abroad. He probably felt he was owed some special attention. And she was only too happy to give it to him.

'OK. I'm all yours. I'll just change into something more appropriate for my unexpected holiday.' She turned towards the stairs then swung round to face him again. If she didn't get an answer to the niggling question in her mind it could ruin their whole day. 'Brad. Did you buy the Hall?' Sally wasn't even aware she was holding her breath as she waited for his answer.

'No! Chris did,' Brad laughed.

Sally let her breath out with a whoosh of satisfaction and hurried up the stairs. She couldn't say really why it was so important Brad wasn't the owner of the Hall, and working out the reason didn't matter now anyway, did it?

They had a magical day. Brad drove them to their favourite pub, where he parked the car, and they strolled for miles along the river path. Their talk ranged through all the usual topics lovers discuss with such earnest attention, favourite things, childhood memories, best and worst experiences. Their exchanges were punctuated by laughter, companionable silences, and the kind of kisses that just touched base, when they could no longer resist the urge to proclaim their love, gentle kisses, full of promise for the future, and plans for a more intimate setting.

They returned to the pub for lunch and spent the next few hours beside the roaring fire in the almost deserted bar. The landlord told them it would liven up later, as folk came in to begin their weekends with a relaxing pint. Sally and Brad exchanged private smiles and assured him it was fine just as it was.

When Sally looked at her watch and made a move to leave, Brad stayed her with a hand on her arm.

'Sally, my darling, I know you have to get back for the kids, but could we have the rest of the weekend? Just for us? I'm sure Bob could cope for once. I could book us into a lovely country hotel, where you could be pampered and cosseted – by me most of all – and you wouldn't have to lift a finger. There'd be no one to disturb us, day or night,' he finished persuasively. His gentle fingertip made tiny circles on the sensitive skin of the inside of Sally's wrist.

Sally shuddered as a sudden wave of desire ran through her. Firmly she removed his hand and tried to think coherently. She longed to be alone with Brad. The idea of a weekend together filled her mind with wonderful pictures. She blushed as her imaginings became more detailed and dragged her thoughts back to the present. Today had been wonderful but . . . But what? But it hadn't been perfect. There were too many small things throughout the day which had pricked Sally's bubble of contentment. Would it be better to sort them out before they became misunderstandings? She smiled.

'I think that's a wonderful idea. But leave the location to me. No.' she added as Brad would have argued. She put her finger on his lips. 'Not a word. You'll like it. I promise.'

And with that he had to be content.

Bob was more than willing to look after his children on his own.

'About time you had a break from us, love. You go on and enjoy yourselves.'

The children were less easy to appease. Why couldn't they come too? Where was Sally going? Why was she going away?

'To get some peace and quiet for a change,' she laughed. She had agreed with Bob that no-one should be told she was spending the weekend with Brad. After all it was no-one else's business. But the children could well chatter about it in all innocence.

By the time she had tucked them both up for the night it was dark outside, just as Sally had planned. None of the neighbours saw her load her car, and there was no-one near the lodge to see Brad carrying his weekend case to join her. He held out his hand for the car keys, but Sally laughed and shook her head.

'Oh, no. You were in charge this morning. Now it's my turn.'

A swift frown crossed his face, to be replaced by an indulgent smile as he allowed her to escort him to the passenger side of her car.

When she stopped the car outside her flat in Libchester, Brad groaned.

'Not more trouble with the obnoxious Clarks, I hope?'

'No fear. I got shot of them long ago, when you were away. Come on.'

Burdened with her case and several packages, some of which she loaded on to Brad, Sally led the way up the path, through the hall, and down the stairs to number 15A. Once the front door was opened, she dumped her load, turned up the thermostat, and went through the flat, switching on table lamps until the whole apartment was bathed in soft light. That done she unwrapped the large bunch of flowers she had picked in the cottage garden and divided them between three vases.

All this time Brad watched her with a smile on his lips. At last, as she placed the last vase on top of a carved bookcase, he caught her arm.

'Hey,' he said softly. 'Hello. I'm here. When you've stopped playing house, I want to kiss you.'

Sally went willingly into his arms. It was some time before she remembered the butter and other groceries rapidly heating up on the kitchen unit.

'You're a bad influence on me Brad Picton,' she laughed, looking lovingly up into his face. 'Whenever you are near me, all rational thought goes out of the window.'

'Good.' He was unrepentant but let her go long enough for her to rescue their food for the next two days.

Safe from prying eyes and interruptions Sally and Brad continued to explore each other mentally, physically and emotionally. Brad discovered Sally could never kill a spider but had to catch it in a jar and put it out into the garden. Sally discovered Brad was amazingly ignorant of all growing things as they tackled the small garden outside the French windows. She rescued more than one of her precious plants from his 'weeding' and felt it safer to let him wield a spade in a firmly restricted area.

Brad had been amazed at the transformation of the flat.

'I don't remember it being as nice as this last time we were here,' he puzzled, looking round the freshly painted walls, the gleaming furniture and the fresh curtains at the windows.

'I should think not. Once I'd got shot of the Clarks, I couldn't bear the thought they had been here. I wanted to erase all trace, so I redecorated the whole place, and bought some new pieces of furniture. Chris was a great help. Once he knew what he was supposed to be doing. He is such a fool,' she laughed affectionately.

She didn't see the shutter go down on Brad's face, rendering it hard and unyielding, but she heard the note in his voice as he quizzed her.

'Chris? What's it got to do with him? You must have spent a lot of time together to do this much decorating?' Was there a strange emphasis on the last word?

Sally pushed away his arms and swung around from her position, cuddled on the settee with her back to Brad's chest.

'What's that supposed to mean? I thought Chris was your friend? Didn't you tell me to trust him?'

'You may trust him, to help or give advice. But I don't trust him around women.' Brad growled.

'Why?'

'He's pinched too many of my girlfriends in the past.'

'As you pinched his, he says.'

'That's right. But they didn't matter. You're different. And if I thought he . . . he and you.'

Sally shoved his arms away and jumped to her feet, her eyes shooting sparks of rage. 'Now you stop. You stop right there. How dare you. Is that what you think of me? You're away for a few weeks, so of course I'll have a fling with your friend, your best friend?'

Brad gaped at the towering fury who stood in front of him with her hands clenched into fists. Was she going to hit him? The thought made him smile. Big mistake.

'Oh, that's funny, is it? Well, I don't think so. Chris did try to flirt with me once, but as soon as I explained how things were with us, he stopped and never put a foot wrong again. You may not trust your friend, Brad, but I thought you trusted me. Oh, no. Of course you don't, do you? I'm the one who has to be kept in the dark.' Tears of anger sparkled on Sally's lashes as she turned away and stomped off into the kitchen.

Brad groaned. Were they back to square one? Had he blown it all over again? He followed Sally into the kitchen and set about repairing the damage.

He succeeded in the end and harmony was restored. He apologised for his jealousy. He'd never known he could be jealous. No-one else had ever mattered to him the way Sally did. His jealousy had been a surprise to him too, and one he hadn't handled well. His abject contrition melted Sally's heart. His explanations soothed the hurt she had felt at his mistrust, but it cast a little shadow on her happiness. She thrust it away and threw herself into enjoyment of these magical stolen hours they had together.

Brad's total concentration and undeniable love filled every moment. Whatever they might be doing, it needed only a certain exchanged look and they were in each others arms. Brad couldn't get enough of Sally's kisses. They went to his head until all rational thought was gone. He worshipped her body with awe until his rising passion swept them both to undreamed of heights. Brad's naked chest was a magnet for Sally's caressing fingers. The sight of Sally walking round the flat nude, save for his own shirt made Brad groan and reach for her again. The hours passed so quickly it was a shock to realise it was Sunday evening. They must return to the village.

'But it won't be for long will it, my darling? We'll soon be married, won't we? Next week? Would that be long enough for you to get a pretty dress? I can drive you up to London tomorrow. We'll stay at my flat there and I'll get a Special Licence. I suppose you want to get married in the village church? I'll see the vicar first thing in the morning. It will be wonderful, my Sally. Lucy will like to be a bridesmaid, won't she, but I'm not sure about

Philip. Not a page boy, I think. What about chief usher? I'd be happy for him to be my best man, but I suppose I should ask Chris to do the honours. After all we've helped each other out of so many scrapes. What do you think? Next week? Or the week after? I won't wait much longer than that. I can't bear to let you out of my sight. My darling Sally. You've changed my life. I never knew I could be so happy.' The words tumbled out. Brad's eyes shone with enthusiasm as he made his plans.

'No, Brad.'

'No what?'

'No, Brad, I won't marry you next week, or the week after.' At the sight of Brad's stricken face, Sally nearly wavered. But she was fighting for her future happiness. She had to get it right now. She nerved herself for battle and went on in a low voice. 'I won't marry you at all . . . yet.'

Chapter Seventeen

The colour drained from Brad's face, leaving it a sickly yellow where the last of his tan lingered. He shook his head, lost and bewildered.

'Sally?' he whispered. 'I thought you loved me, as I love you.'

Sally looked at him with anguished eyes. It would be so easy to give in, to cradle his head against her breast and promise to do anything that would make him happy. But how long would that happiness last? She knew herself too well. She bit her lip, swallowed and tried to stop her voice shaking.

'Brad, I do love you. And I want to marry you, but not yet. Please sit down and listen and I'll try to explain.'

Numbly, still confused, but clinging to the lifeline of her declared love, Brad let himself be led to the settee.

Sally took a deep breath and began. 'I love you more than I ever thought it possible to love anyone. I love you and I want to marry you, but I want you to ask me.'

'I just did!'

'No, Brad. You *told* me. You said we'd soon be married and then went on to *tell* me what would happen between now and then. I think you did offer me the option of next week or the week after and generously allowed me to decide if I really wanted to be married in the village church, but that was all.' She cocked her head and gave him a half-smile, waiting for his reaction.

'But, Sally, darling. This is silly. You've said you want to marry me so what's the problem? I don't understand.'

'No, you don't, do you,' she said sadly. 'That *is* the problem. I've been organising my life for a long time now, and Dad's and the children's, since Sharon left.'

'I know, my poor darling, but that's all over. You have me now and I'll take care of you.'

Sally jumped up and turned on him as she had before. 'Why won't you listen!' she shouted.

Brad was hurt. 'I do listen.'

'You may listen, but you don't hear then,' Sally raged. 'You're like a bulldozer. You flatten everything in your path. And don't laugh. It's not funny. I don't want to be taken care of. I'm not a child and I'm not helpless and I'm perfectly capable of making my own decisions.'

'Of course you are.'

'There you go again. You say that and yet you don't mean it.'

'Of course I do.'

'There's no, of course, about it.'

'Look, Sally, you're obviously upset. Let's calm down and see what the problem is. Then we can sort it all out.' Brad said soothingly. Bad move.

'You're the problem.' Sally gritted her teeth. 'Can't you hear how patronising you sound? I appreciate, Brad, that most of your life you've had to look out for other people, first your mother, and then, no doubt, your employees. No! Don't say anything. I'm sure you've always done what's best for them. But you've done the best that *you* thought they deserved. Did you ever ask them what they wanted? I'm not your mother, I'm not an employee and I can think for myself. I don't need you to make every decision in life for me. Next you'll be telling me what to wear.'

'Now that's silly. I don't know what you're talking about.'

'I'm talking about the fact that I'm a big girl now. I don't *need* looking after. I can take of myself, and I *need* to make decisions for myself about *my* life. I don't want to be another *thing* you have to be responsible for in your busy working day.' Sally paused a moment to collect her thoughts. This time Brad was silent. Perhaps, at last, he realised whatever Sally was saying was very important for them both. She sat down on a low chair, a little way away from him, and tried to explain.

'You said I'm different to all the other girlfriends you've had. How?'

'That's easy. I didn't love them.'

'But that's not the only difference is it? They were probably as widely travelled as you. Perhaps they were as rich as you and moved in the world of society entertaining? I'm sure they wore designer clothes and dropped everything if you wanted to take them out?

'I must have a great deal of novelty value. Apart from a school exchange trip to France and a holiday with a friend in Majorca, I've never been out of the British Isles. I'm a country girl and, moreover, one with ties you've never come across. A novelty for someone you were dating, not to be permanently available, if Chris is to be believed. You even thought I was the children's mother for a while. Did that intrigue you?' She hung her head for a moment to gather all her courage. Was she doing the stupidest thing she had ever done in her life?

'I don't want to be a novelty, Brad. I want our love to last. I don't want to be a responsibility or someone you have to take care of. I want to be your partner, your equal partner. If you were thinking of domestic little Sally waiting patiently at home with your pipe and slippers, you can forget it. I want to see the world, Brad. I want to travel with you. I want you to show me the wonderful places you've been and the marvels you've seen. I want to be with you, wherever you are, sharing every part of your life. I'm happy for you to teach me, Brad. There's so much I don't know. But it must be as an equal, or our life together won't work.'

She waited, scarcely daring to breathe. What would Brad's reaction be? Finally, as the silence stretched out she could bear it no longer. With anxious pleading eyes she looked across at Brad. His elbows rested on his knees, his head was in his hands. When he finally looked up his expression was haggard.

'Have I blown it? I feel as though you've cast me adrift. I've always known what to do and say. I've learned the hard way. But it's got to the stage, I suppose, where no-one would dare to contradict me. Whatever I said was accepted as fact. Until a red-haired youngster in shorts and scruffy trainers told me where to get off.' The ghost of a smile crossed his face at the memory. 'You've never been afraid to speak your mind to me, have you? It's one of the refreshing things I love about you. Farthing is the only other person who can keep me in line, now that Jock and Mother have gone. But Farthing doesn't tease me the way you do, with that imp of mischief in your eyes which can always make me smile, no matter how mad you're making me. You're right. I have ordered my life and the lives of others for so long I don't know any other way to live.

But I'll try. You say I can teach you, but you must teach me, Sally. Teach me how to be a reasonable human being. According to you, I don't know how.'

'That's not true. You're wonderful with the children. They adore you.'

'Children are easy. I just talk to them as friends, but if I suggest something, they obey without question, don't they? So what am I doing wrong with you, the one person I want to make happy?'

Sally sighed. Did they really have to go through this, blow by blow? Apparently they did. Brad wasn't used to living with anyone else, particularly anyone whose wishes he needed to consider.

'Right.' Sally sat up straight and prepared to educate Brad. 'Let's go through this weekend. First you rang Miss Penney and told her I wouldn't be in to work.'

'What's wrong with that? We wanted to spend the day together, didn't we? Didn't you enjoy it?'

'You know I enjoyed it. That's not the question. You had no right to take a decision like that for me without so much as a by-your-leave. Had you suggested we spend the day together I was perfectly capable of telephoning Miss Penney myself. She'd hardly refuse me, knowing who I'd be spending my time with, would she?' Sally grimaced. 'But that's another story.

'I have my job at the Hall and I'm good at it. I am conscientious and take my work seriously. It is not up to you to decide off your own bat when I will and will not turn up for work. Just now you spoke of . . . no . . . you *told* me you were going to take me up to London tomorrow. Another day off work? And when we got to the pub, you didn't ask me what I wanted to drink.'

'But you always have a Spritzer.'

'Just because on the few occasions we've been out together I have drunk Spritzers, it doesn't mean I don't occasionally like to drink something else. I wasn't given the opportunity. You *decided* we would sit at the table by the fire. You *decided* we didn't want a dessert. You *decided* we would have coffee. My wishes were never consulted. When we were coming to the flat, you almost took the huff when I wouldn't hand over my car keys. *My* car keys, please note. You hate not being in control of everything. Stop for a minute and think of yourself in my place, having decisions, even silly little personal ones, made for you. Don't you understand?'

Brad's expression was rueful. 'But you do like Spritzers and I know you don't eat dessert at lunchtime, so what was so bad about catering for your tastes?'

'My tastes, as you put it, are not set in stone. I might like to eat or drink something else for a change. I'd like the choice to be offered.'

'Okay. I'll try and remember. Sorry, I *will* remember,' he added as he saw the look on Sally's face. 'But you don't mean it about not marrying me, do you? Please, Sally, don't do that to me.' His voice had lost the light tone of his previous remarks. This struck to his heart. 'I thought no-one could ever fill that void I've carried around in me all my life. I knew it was there, but I didn't know what it was. You taught me it was the absence of love. Now you've filled me with your love, please don't take it away and leave me empty again. They say what you've never known you'll never miss. I know what it is to love and be loved by you, my darling. You're my reason for living. Without your love now, I wouldn't know how to go on.'

'Don't say that, Brad,' Sally cried. 'Of course I love you, more than life itself. I'm fighting for our future.'

'Fighting? Fighting me?'

'No. I'm fighting myself, and my longing to throw myself into your arms and forget everything else. This is hurting me too. I hate to be at odds with you over anything. If I didn't believe it was vital, I wouldn't ask it of you.'

The sadness in her face was heartrending. Finally Brad realised their only hope of lasting happiness was to hold back his domineering character and give Sally the respect she deserved as an intelligent, competent adult perfectly capable of running her own life – even without him. The thought made him shudder. He'd do anything, anything at all not to lose Sally, his love, the only woman in the world who could make his life complete.

Chapter Eighteen

They drove back to the village in a thoughtful mood. As Brad said goodnight to Sally, she thought she had never known such yearning in a kiss. There was no doubt Brad loved, wanted and needed her. The future *must* come right for them. If only he was prepared to let her into his head, as completely as his heart, all would be well.

As she carried her case through the cottage door, she heard Bob's voice on the telephone. He sounded amused.

'That's alright then. I'll leave them out for you, but you'd better get them back before church on Sunday . . . yes, usually . . . especially in cold weather. Right. I must go. Bye.'

He smiled as Sally kissed him hello and asked after the children who were in bed.

'They wanted to wait up for you, but as I had no idea when you'd be back I had to put my foot down. Had a good time?' His question was perfectly normal, but the hint of laughter in his eyes puzzled Sally. He almost looked as if he was hiding a secret.

'Yes, thanks. Lovely, but I must get my stuff ready for work tomorrow, so I'll go up. 'Night Dad.'

Before she slept that night Sally gazed up at the moon and prayed all would be well. She had fallen in love with Brad so quickly, so deeply. Surely he couldn't turn out to be a domineering stranger; someone she couldn't live with? He acted out of habit. Well, habits could be broken, with good will and especially with love.

Brad had asked Sally if he might walk her to work next day.

'I have to go to the Hall to see Farthing, so if it's alright with you, we could go together?' One eyebrow rose as he waited for her answer.

Sally's heart had turned over and a heat suffused her blood. Just so had he looked before taking her to bed at the flat. She swallowed and tried to control her ragged breathing.

'Lovely,' she'd managed to squeak, before leaping back into the car and driving home.

As they walked through the crisp Autumn morning side by side, Sally remembered what she had intended asking Brad over the weekend, before other things occupied her mind. She couldn't stop a smile on her lips as she thought of those 'other things'. She turned to Brad.

'What's Chris going to do with the Hall?'

'Chris? What do you mean?'

'Well now he's bought it, what's he going to do with it? Lindsey Enterprises don't use more than a few rooms, so what plans has he got for the rest?'

Brad stopped and looked puzzled. 'Chris doesn't own the Hall. I do. Whatever gave you the idea he owned it?'

Sally's eyes were huge. 'You did. You told me he bought it. Then I went and got changed and other things took over. That was the end of the conversation. I don't understand.'

Brad tucked his hand through her arm. 'Let's keep walking. It's a nice day but too cold to hang around. And you may be late for work,' he added with a grin. 'Remember I told you how Adrian hated me. He did all sorts to stop me buying shares in Jock's companies. That wasn't too difficult to get around. I bought some stock through companies and got friends to buy for me and then sell to my holding company. Adrian managed to block several purchases by finding out about my business interests. There was no way he would have sold the Hall to me, or any of my friends. Chris was the perfect answer.'

'But Chris is your best friend.'

'Yes. But Adrian didn't know that. Chris is not a good correspondent. He never worked for Jock, and he has been out of the country for years. So Chris bought the Hall.'

'Is he rich then?'

Brad laughed. 'Money and Chris don't stay together long. That's why I paid him for his services with shares which will bring him in an income. He doesn't know yet, so not a word.'

'How does he think you paid him?'

'He'd have a fit if I offered him money for a favour. I gave him the money to buy the Hall, or rather, I had it transferred to his account from a source Adrian wouldn't query. Then I bought the Hall from Chris for a pound.'

Sally laughed. 'A pound? Really?'

'Yes. All perfectly legal and above board.'

'So Adrian was defeated and you own the Hall.'

By this time they had reached the side entrance Sally always used. Brad held the door open for her. He smiled down at her with that special warmth in his eyes he showed to her, and her alone. His voice was gentle and intimate as he answered her.

'I told you I'd almost decided to make my home here. I think it would be a wonderful place for children to grow up. Don't you?'

There were stars in Sally's eyes and her cheeks were flushed as she booted up her computer and tried to settle her mind to the jobs awaiting her attention. She had enough to keep her busy all morning.

At lunchtime Brad put his head around the door and asked if she would like to join him at the pub for lunch. Sally hid a smile and said she'd be delighted. She wasn't smiling when Brad told her he had to go up to London in the afternoon.

'I should be back tomorrow. I'll phone you this evening and tell how I've got on.'

'What are you laughing at?'

'Me? I'm not laughing. I'm just happy to be with you,' Brad answered with an injured air and took a pull at his pint.

Sally frowned. True, Brad wasn't laughing, but there seemed to be an air of suppressed excitement about him. He said nothing about marriage, nor did he press Sally to reassure him again of her love. That should be a good thing. Shouldn't it?

That evening, true to his word, Brad phoned and promised to return next day. After she hung up, Sally felt restless. She had finished her chores in the afternoon. It was too dark to do any gardening. The children went quietly to bed. There was nothing to distract Sally from her feeling of emptiness. She'd told Brad she needed to make her own decisions, lead her own life and yet here she was, totally at a loose end because he was away. How completely he had become an essential part of her life. No, she corrected herself. He was *the* essential part of her life and without him her existence would be an empty shell. She jumped, when the phone rang again. It was Chris.

'Hi there, lovely Sally. Haven't seen you for yonks. How about coming for a drink with me down at the pub? I know Brad's away this evening. He's hogged your company so much I haven't set eyes on either of you since he's been back. Until today, that is, when I saw him briefly.'

As always Sally felt Chris was a link with Brad. Anything was better than fidgeting around the cottage until bedtime, so she agreed to meet him in the lounge bar. The Snug or Public Bar would be too full of her friends and acquaintances to have a proper conversation and there were questions Sally wanted answered.

'Brad told me how you helped him buy the Hall.'

Chris grinned. 'Yes. I really enjoyed stopping Adrian's little red wagon – the bastard. Sorry! But he is. If I could get my hands on him for a quiet half hour.' Suddenly his pleasant face looked grim. Sally was intrigued.

'Why?'

'Can you ask? Twice he tried, and nearly succeeded in murdering Brad.'

Sally's face paled. Of course Brad had told her of the so-called accidents, which had befallen him. He'd said Adrian wanted to murder him but, unfortunately, that was a phrase all too often used without meaning behind it. I could murder a drink. I'd like to murder him. How often had she heard someone say things like that? So she hadn't perhaps taken the words literally, despite his adventures in Paraguay. She'd been more concerned at the effects of malaria on her dear love. Suddenly the harsh reality of Brad's escapes from death came home to her. She gulped and shivered.

'I never realised just how dangerous it was,' she whispered.

'Hey, I'm sorry. I didn't mean to frighten you. It's all over now and Adrian's behind bars. For a long time to come. I gather you had something to do with collecting evidence against him? Clever girl.' Chris turned Sally thoughts away from what might have been.

'It was like looking for a needle in a haystack, or in a maze rather. Peeling an onion might be a better way to describe it. A thread went from one company to another which hid another and so on.' She laughed. 'Don't let me get started on the excitement of auditing detective work or we'll be here all night.'

Chris gave her an appraising look. 'You're good at your job, aren't you? Will you give it up when you and Brad get married.'

Sally froze. What had Brad been saying? He'd seen Chris today. Surely he wasn't trying to force her hand by broadcasting his plans to all and sundry? Hadn't he taken in anything of what she had said?

'Now what have I said to make you look like that?' Chris went on. 'You are going to marry him, aren't you?' His voice took on a more serious note. 'You told me you loved him, Sally. Please don't say you've changed your mind. I've never seen Brad like this before. He's so happy, he's almost human. He actually asked Farthing today if she would like a tea dispenser installed in the office.'

Sally relaxed and hid a smile. Well done, Brad. A beginning at least. Perhaps he had taken to heart her plea to consider other's wishes.

'I think he'd forgotten she's got a housekeeper who can make tea for her any time. Brad always drinks coffee at work, but Farthing prefers tea. He's never bothered to ask her preference before in all the years she's worked for him. Amazing! And another thing.' Chris was well into his stride by now. 'He asked her when she wanted to take her holidays. In the past she's always had to fit her time off around his needs. Sometimes she's cancelled her plans at the last minute. It's not that he's a slave-driver, but he relies on her so much she lets him ride roughshod over her own arrangements.'

'So she's her own worst enemy,' put in Sally. 'It's just as much her fault as Brad's. She wouldn't like to feel she was anything but indispensable.'

Chris grinned. 'You're right there. She's as bad at delegating as he is.'

'Enough of all that. Let's talk about something else,' smiled Sally. 'What are you going to do with yourself when your leave's up? Do you still want to rent my flat in Libchester?'

'I should say so. I'm going to work for Brad. Didn't he tell you?'

'No.' Sally didn't say that Chris and his future had not been on their private agenda in the time she and Brad had spent together. But she hugged the memory of those precious hours to her heart. 'What are you going to do?'

'Not sure really yet. We haven't dotted the i's and crossed the t's but I think it will be a sort of roving commission. Something like the job Brad used to do for Jock.'

'But Jock had a business empire, didn't he? Would there be enough work to keep you busy full time? And would you like that kind of thing?'

Chris looked at Sally with a crooked smile on his face. 'Yeah. I'd like it. It would be just up my street. Until I meet someone like you and get the urge to settle down just as Brad has, his old kind of life is fine by me. Sally, how much do you know about Brad's business?'

'Nothing really. He said he was financially well-off when Jock died, and I know he's been able to buy out Adrian. I suppose that's used up most of his money but given him assets in its place. And then he's bought the Hall, so I suppose ready money could be quite tight now.'

Chris grinned. 'Brad bought the Hall with pocket-money,' he scoffed. 'True, Adrian cost him a packet, but no more than he could afford. And now he's got control, the companies will make fat profits again. They are all solid business which just need running competently.' He watched in amusement the meaning of his words penetrate Sally's mind.

'You mean he's really wealthy?' she asked finally.

'Let's just say he counts his millions in double figures,' Chris agreed.

Sally's eyes matched the perfect O which was her mouth as she struggled to believe Chris wasn't joking. No wonder Brad had such a habit of command if he had to keep such a huge concern running smoothly. As the implications of what she had heard sank in, new worries sprang up in Sally's mind. Would the love she had to offer Brad be enough for him? She had spoken rather disparagingly about the Society women he used to date,

180

thinking of them as lightweight, social butterflies encountered in infrequent leisure time. But this wealth of his would make them and their kind the more usual company for a man in his position. Would Little Mithering and the day-to-day doings of village life become irksome now Brad was fit and healthy, ready for the challenges of his far-reaching concerns?

When she voiced these thoughts to Chris he laughed away her fears.

'You must be joking. That was never Brad's kind of life. Sure, occasionally we did hit the high spots, usually together, all very light-hearted. You won't see his name in the gossip columns or his face in the glossies. He doesn't run racehorses or have a fancy yacht. Although,' he added, 'come to think of it, now he wants to settle down, maybe he'll go in for that sort of thing. I've never been to Ascot. It might be fun to get up a party. You could wear one of those incredible creations on your head that I've seen the women wearing on the telly.' His smile was infectious.

Sally appreciated him trying to cheer her up, but she knew so little of Brad's other life, his life before he turned up at the lodge.

'What's Brad doing in London, Chris?' she asked suddenly. She couldn't miss the alarm which flared in his eyes.

Swiftly he schooled his features and shrugged. 'The usual things, I suppose, tending to business. Come on, are you ready for the other half?'

As she watched him weave his way through the other drinkers to a space at the bar, Sally wished she could banish this feeling that once again people were hiding things from her. She was being kept in the dark and she didn't like it. She didn't like it one bit.

Chapter Nineteen

Next day Sally worked with a smile on her face and a glow in her eyes. Each time she thought of Brad's return that evening a thrill ran through her. She laughed at herself. He'd been away less than twenty-four hours. But when she recalled the feel of his body pressed against hers and the sensual mastery of his lips, her bones turned to water. She wondered how she could possibly last until she could be in his arms again. She was mad. Mad to keep them waiting for something they both longed for. As soon as he got back, she would tell him she'd marry him tomorrow if that's what he wanted.

He arrived in time to share an evening meal with the family at the cottage. His hungry eyes followed Sally's every move. Never had she felt so clumsy. Twice she nearly dropped a plate and Lucy was only saved from having a shower of hot peas tipped over her by Brad's swift action. As he rescued the bowl from Sally, their fingers touched. Electricity shot up her arm and set alarm bells ringing. Every nerve ending sprang to life. She gazed at Brad with naked longing in her eyes. He could have drowned in their depths as they stood, side by side, yet so enmeshed in their love they were one entity.

Bob's smile was indulgent. 'Don't you think it might be better to eat the peas hot?' he enquired slyly.

'I don't like peas, anyway,' piped up Lucy.

'Yuk! Cold peas,' was Philip's contribution.

The little exchange gave Sally and Brad a chance to pull themselves together. The meal passed off pleasantly as Brad answered the children's questions about London. He promised to take them on the London Eye. They must ask Sally and Bob when it would suit them and they would have a family day out. Discussion of the Eye, Madame Tussaud's, the Tower of London and a boat trip on the Thames occupied them until bedtime. Sally and Brad escaped as the children went up for their baths.

'Poor old Chris had better move into your flat,' laughed Brad as he unlocked the door of the lodge. 'I'm not sure if he's with Farthing this evening or down at the pub. He was just invited to make himself scarce.'

Sally smiled. Just what she wanted, Brad all to herself in peace and privacy.

When they next came up for air, Sally was rosy cheeked. As always, her bones had melted at Brad's touch. He had branded her willing body with a trail of fiery kisses as she squirmed beneath him, pressing herself deeper into his embrace.

As her heart slowed its racing pace, she waited for him to sweep her up in his arms and carry her into the bedroom. With her head nestled against his naked chest she could hear the thunder of Brad's heart and knew he too longed to complete their reunion. But he sat back in the depths of the sagging settee and cuddled her into a more comfortable position.

Sally frowned. What was wrong? Why was Brad settling down here?

'Brad? Is everything alright?' She turned her face up to him.

He looked at her with eyes whose inner fires were only just banked down, only just under control. He smiled and kissed her forehead.

'I promised myself I wouldn't make love to you again until my ring was on your finger,' he said with a rueful smile. 'I am trying to change my ways my darling; trying to give other people space and that includes you. I am practising holding back instead of going ahead and taking what I want when I want it. You have no idea how hard that promise is to keep.'

'Don't bet on it,' replied Sally with feeling. 'What makes you think you're the biggest loser from that?' She gave his shoulder a gentle punch to underline her frustration. 'I wanted to talk to you about that waiting business, Brad. You see I only intend to get married once, and I wanted, very selfishly, to enjoy the whole thing. You know, the engagement, introducing you to all my friends, showing off this great sexy hunk I've caught for myself, making all the girls jealous; then planning our wedding together. But if you want it, I'll marry you tomorrow. I love you so much.'

Passion flared again in Brad's eyes at her words. He folded her in his arms and held her close. 'My darling Sally, you don't know what it means to hear you say that. But you're right. We're only going to do this once, so we'll have the lot. I do want to meet your friends. Most of my guests will come under the heading of business acquaintances rather than chums. It will be good to have a few friendly faces among the crowd. Do you think I'll pass muster?'

'Fishing for compliments, are we?' Sally laughed and had to spend some time showing Brad just how much she thought he would be acceptable to her judgmental friends.

'You shall have whatever you want for our wedding,' Brad promised. 'I'd like to give you the moon and stars.'

'Chris told me how rich you really are. I had no idea. But even for you, my darling, I think the moon might be a bit out of reach. Besides, other lovers must want it left in the sky, to wish on just as we do.'

Brad was amused. He shrugged. 'So the cat's out of the bag, is it? I wondered how long it would be until the penny dropped. But the money, as money isn't important to me, only what it can achieve,' he went on earnestly. 'I told you I managed to give Mum some comfort before she died, but since then I've had no-one to spend it on. Spending is another habit I intend to acquire - like listening to people,' he finished with a wicked grin.

'I heard you shocked Miss Penney with your consideration.'

Brad groaned. 'Can a man do nothing without the whole world knowing? You're right, though, she was shocked. I think she thought I'd lost the plot. I've been thinking over what you said, and I realise just how it's come about - too little time to get things done and an absolute idea of what was necessary. But I've made a start to reform, and you must remind me if I slip up. I want your happiness more than anything in the world, my love. You're all I've got now Mum has gone.'

'What about your father?' queried Sally gently. 'Did you ever find out what happened to him?'

Brad's face became grim. 'Oh, yes. As soon as the money piled up, he came out of the woodwork, just like the low-life termite he is.'

'Termite's are very hard-working,' Sally ventured to lighten his mood, but his laugh in reply was short and ugly.

'Don't compare the two then. I almost didn't agree to see him when he turned up at my office, after a newspaper article in the Financial Times mentioned me as being one of the wealthiest men in the country. It was sheer curiosity, I suppose, that made me agree to see him in the end. I'd remembered him as a big man, shouting at me and intimidating my mother.' He gave another ugly laugh. 'What a difference. His shrunken bravado was just a shell of my memories, but I could still see traces of the bully in him.

'He started off with the old long-lost son routine. I don't suppose he even realised that at seven years old, children can remember, especially bad things. When that didn't work, he changed to bluster. He was my father. I owed him my existence, and all that crap. After that, it was a descent into whining self-pity. Things had gone wrong for him. Nothing was his fault. You know the kind of thing.' Brad's lip curled in disgust at the memory.

'So what happened?'

'I would probably have given him something, just to get rid of him. But he made the mistake of bringing my mother into the conversation. He blamed his departure on her. She'd been a useless wife and driven him away. That did it. I sent him off with a flea in his ear. Security escorted him out of the building. Then my solicitor went after him and impressed upon him I was not a good candidate for blackmail or public pressure. If he went to the Press with any '*millionaire's father exists on the poverty line*' nonsense, he'd come off worst. I had nothing to hide and plenty of power to sue him for defamation of character.'

'Would you have done that?' Sally was intrigued.

Brad laughed again, but this time with a little humour. 'Probably not. I couldn't be bothered. But I didn't need to. He got the message.'

'And that's the last time you saw him?'

'Yes.'

'I wonder what became of him?'

'I know exactly what became of him, where he is and what he does.'

Sally raised her eyebrows. 'You've kept in touch?'

'No. I just pay someone to watch him, to see he has a roof over his head and enough money to feed himself. I get regular reports. Having money does have its advantages. '

'So do you send him anything?'

'No way. I want no contact at all. When he loses his job, which happens fairly regularly, I make sure another one turns up before he is totally destitute or homeless. He has no idea I'm involved.'

Sally studied Brad's face. He seemed perfectly indifferent to his father's fate. But that wasn't true. From the shadows, he was making sure his father could survive.

'Why do you do it?'

Brad shrugged. 'It costs me nothing, only money. There's no emotion involved, and no guilt. Because one day my mother loved him, I do it for her. I don't even know if she would want me to. All I do know is that as long as he is not destitute, I don't have to think about him. And he won't be on the wedding invitation list,' he finished with a teasing smile.

Sally's heart swelled anew. The more she discovered about this man to whom she had given her heart, the more she loved him. His father had treated him so badly, yet he hadn't turned his back on him. She marvelled at Brad's generous nature.

'I wish I'd met your mother,' she said softly. 'She must have been a remarkable woman to imbue her son with such moral values when life had been so hard and unfair to her. I'm sure she was so proud of the way you turned out. She did a good job on you.'

Brad's eyes shone with love. 'She was remarkable and wonderful, and I know she is happy I've met a woman like her. I never believed it to be possible. But you won't have to struggle as she did, my darling. At last I've found a use for my money.'

'Race horses and yachts?' asked Sally with a grin.

'As many as you like,' assured Brad and sealed his promise with a kiss.

When she could speak again, Sally assured him that horses and boats were not at the top of her wish list. 'Perhaps children?' she suggested. 'One of each to start with. A boy for me and a girl for you. Then you'd really learn how to spoil someone,' she laughed, thinking of an adoring Brad with his own little princess. 'You'd have a permanent account with Hamley's, I bet. But I would like Lindsey Enterprises to move out if we're going to live at the Hall.'

Brad frowned. 'Surely there's room for a couple of offices, without cramping our style? If you really mean it, I suppose I could convert part of the stable block,' he thought aloud.

'Why can't they just go somewhere else?'

'Sending me away from my own house, are you, darling? I don't want to go too far away when I must work.'

'I don't understand. What have you got to do with Lindsey Enterprises? Of course, Miss Penney works for them, doesn't she? Have you got shares in that company too?'

Brad shook his head. 'I know I asked Farthing and Chris not to tell you of our connection in the beginning,' he said, a look of amusement on his face, 'but I never realised how close-mouthed they could be. Did you really not make the connection between me and Lindsey Enterprises?'

'No. Miss Penney spoke of the Chairman, but I don't know his name, or how you are involved with him.'

'I am the Chairman. I am Lindsey Enterprises.'

Sally's mouth dropped open. She'd have to get an automatic closure fitted if Brad kept coming up with such surprises. She blinked. 'Why not Picton Enterprises? What's the secret?'

'That was for Adrian's benefit. I needed a new company, not connected with any of my other ventures. So I chose my mother's name, Lindsey, and used it for a holding company while I fought Adrian. I was sure she'd approve.'

'That reminds me, Brad. I asked Miss Penney for an appointment with the Chairman. Of course! That was when you were in the forest,' she exclaimed. 'She said he was abroad. No wonder she looked so strained. She didn't know where you were. But she did know about the first attack and how ruthless Adrian could be,' she realised. 'Your poor Farthing was very worried about you Brad. Anyway, there was something I wanted to discuss with the Chairman, that is you, I mean.'

'What's that then, my love?'

'It's about a project . . .'

'No, no, no,' cried Brad. 'No business talk. I've taken off my business head, like Worzel Gummidge. I've got my loving head on now. No work outside office hours. Come here, woman, I haven't kissed you for at least ten minutes.'

Sally's protest was swallowed up in his kiss. She surrendered. Tomorrow was another day. Time enough to worry about Home Park then. After all, the Chairman of Lindsey Enterprises wasn't going anywhere.

Chapter Twenty

'It's perfect,' said Brad with pride as he surveyed the model of the Little Mithering Hall Project standing on its table in Miss Penney's office. 'The cabins are all designed to the highest specifications. They'll be completely fitted out so guests can stay in privacy if they want to. Or, if they prefer, they can dine in the first-class restaurant, or get a snack twenty-four hours a day in the cafeteria, both situated in gardens laid out around the central area.'

'Like room service in an hotel?'

'Exactly. We have fishing and water sports on the lake, indoor and outdoor tennis, ten-pin bowling and a superb swimming pool. You can be pampered in the Health Spa there or play golf over here. And there are wonderful walks all around. We'll provide plenty of employment for locals, from chalet-maids and waiters, to office and garden workers. It will be of real benefit to the community, Sally.' He looked anxiously at her face. Farthing had told him of Sally's horrified reaction at her first sight of the model. 'Do you have a problem with that?'

Sally shook her head. 'Not with giving employment. Of course not. But I don't think you've thought this through.'

Brad's lips tightened and Miss Penney's horrified face should have warned Sally she was skating on thin ice, but she ploughed on.

'If you site the houses, sorry, cabins in the trees of Home Park, they have no access to the village.' She indicated the boundaries of Home Park. 'The whole area is secure, as it was intended to be. All this side, nearest the village is made up of private gardens. There isn't even enough access for a footpath.'

'That doesn't matter,' put in Miss Penney. 'The Hall development is self-supporting.'

'We have done our home-work, Sally,' added Brad. 'My people have done a thorough survey. The cabins will look fabulous nestling between the trees. Can't you just see it?'

'I'm sure they've done a good job, Brad. But from what perspective? Yours or the village's?'

Brad stiffened. His look was wary. He sensed a trap but couldn't see where it could be. 'Mine, of course. But the two interests are joined, aren't they? My development will bring badly needed work to the village.'

'Which will die as a result of your interference. It will simply become a group of cottages where your workers live. It will lose its heart.'

'That's nonsense. You're letting emotion over a few trees cloud your judgement.' Brad was becoming irritated by Sally's continued opposition. Anyone else would have been able to see how good his ideas were. But she wouldn't back down.

'It's fact, not nonsense. Will there be a shop in the development? Perhaps your staff will have a discount to spend there?'

Brad nodded. 'It's possible. We like to reward our loyal staff with benefits.'

'So what happens to Mrs Wilson? Is she supposed to survive on newspaper sales? Or will you have those delivered too? And what about Ted at the pub? Do you really think anyone is going to get in their cars to drive out of the Hall gates then back along the road, into the village they can see from their own doors, just to buy a pint of beer? Of course not. They'll either stay in their cabins and drink, go to the restaurant or, once in their cars, drive farther afield exploring the countryside

'The village has already lost one shop, Brad. You own the building now. It was on the ground floor of the house on the corner of Dog Street. When I was a child, I used to love watching Mr Baron mending the shoes, but where can you find a cobbler now? He sold new shoes too, and the other half of the shop was an ironmongers.

'When Mrs Masterson died, some of the estate workers were laid off. The household staff had gone during her illness, long before, except for her cook and personal maid. A couple of village women did the cleaning, but all the rest left the area. The houses they'd occupied were let out as holiday homes. Those people brought their car boots full of super-market supplies and never patronised the village shops.' Impatiently Sally dashed a tear from her eye as she tried so hard to explain how the village was dying. 'You have the power to turn this around, Brad. You said you wanted to spend your money. Well spend it wisely. Resurrect the village.'

Brad looked at Sally's pleading face. He pursed his lips, swung around and paced to the window. He stood there and looked with unseeing eyes onto the neat beds and immaculate lawns. Then he turned back to the two waiting women and shook his head.

'No. I'm sorry, Sally. I don't see how scrapping this project is going to revitalise your dying village.'

When he'd turned her down, Sally's cheeks went white, then she rallied her arguments again. 'You're doing it again, Brad. Not listening. When have I ever asked you to scrap the project?'

'But you said . . .'

'I asked you to save the Home Park. The project itself sounds wonderful with a few changes here and there.'

Various expressions chased each other across Brad's face. He seemed at first indignant, then surprised, then once again wary.

'Changes?'

'Yes. I've had days to think of this and I may have the answer. If you move the cabins over to here, around the old Home Farm farmhouse, which you can revamp for your administration and catering block, then the barns and outbuildings can be converted for your leisure pursuits.'

'But the golf course is there. The farmhouse was to be the clubhouse,' objected Miss Penney.

'Have you seen it? It's huge. A real old Victorian house, built to accommodate a huge family as well as servants and farm workers. You don't need a clubhouse that size. Put the golf course over here on this area of less fertile land. There are gradients here and some pretty copses of hazel trees where we used to collect nuts. Couldn't they be used as features? The river which feeds the lake runs through there. Don't you need water features on golf courses?'

Brad's smile was now admiring. 'You've really thought this out, haven't you?'

'Of course. The soil round the farmhouse is better so you can plant gardens and trees – ten foot high if you want to. With the cabins over on Home Farm, all you need to reach the village is a feeder road, off the approach, to a new access cut through the perimeter wall. It makes the pub close enough to stroll down to of an evening. An added attraction I would have thought?'

'But what about all the money you've already spent on surveys and plans and models?' Miss Penney was horrified.

'It's only money, Farthing. What else are you supposed to do with it?' Brad smiled at Sally. 'We move the cabins, and you save your trees?'

'Oh, yes, Brad, please,' she beseeched. 'I have a very good reason for wanting them to stay just where they are,' she added in a much lower tone, for his ears only.

Brad didn't ask her reason. Something told him it was very personal. It might have had something to do with the look in Sally's eyes as she gazed at him with such trusting love.

'I'll think about it,' he promised.

That evening Brad took Sally out for dinner.

'It's the only way I can keep my hands off you,' he explained. But the look in his eyes set Sally's blood sizzling.

'If you can do that to me with just a look,' she whispered, 'I think you've got a good idea there. Any more prolonged physical contact and I'll burn up completely, either with passion or, more likely, frustrated desire.'

Fire glowed in Brad's eyes. He reached across the table and lifted Sally's left hand to his lips. He kissed her fingers, bare of rings and smiled to himself.

'Not so long now, my love,' he murmured.

Sally tried to inject a different note into the conversation. 'I thought at the weekend we might go into Libchester and meet the gang, if you'd like that? I can give Libby a 'bell' and ask her to round up some of the others. We can stay at the flat and walk down to the pub. It'll be fun.'

'That sounds fine. I'd enjoy it. You go ahead and make the arrangements and you can tell me what's happening when I phone tomorrow. Don't look like that, my darling. I have to go to London, but I promise I'll be back for the weekend, and I'll bring you something you'll like.'

'I don't need presents, Brad, just you.'

'Dad, if Brad and I were to marry, what would you do about the children?' Sally queried next evening as she waited for the promised telephone call. 'He's talked about making the Hall his headquarters,' she smiled. 'It's a beautiful old house. It would make a lovely home. And it's certainly big enough if you wanted to move in with us.'

'Have you mentioned this possibility to Brad?'

'No, not yet. I've just thought of it. But I'm sure he wouldn't object. You two get on so well together.'

'As friends, yes. But I believe in newly-weds having their own space. It doesn't matter how big the Hall is, I'm sure the last thing Brad would want is his father-in-law and a couple of children under the same roof.'

'But you can't manage the children and your job.'

'No, I can't. Actually Brad and I have discussed this. He offered to replace you with a house-keeper.'

Sally's eyes were round. She didn't know whether to be angry or amused. 'He never said anything to me.'

'Well it doesn't really concern you, does it? They're my children. It's my house, and it's my problem.'

Sally opened her mouth to argue, then closed it again. Dad was right, but there was a small pain of rejection in her heart. Could she be replaced so easily?

'My first thought was to tell Brad I didn't need his charity. Then common sense took over as he explained. You will always come first with us, as with Brad, but he knows all too well how conscientious you are. You'd never go and leave the children unless you were quite happy with whoever takes over your duties. Duties, mark you, not your place. No-one could ever fill that, girl. And you'll only be up at the Hall.'

Sally smiled. 'So what conclusion did you two schemers arrive at?'

'We both want your peace of mind, and the money means nothing to Brad. I swallowed my pride. Brad will pay the wages, and you will choose your successor, when the time comes,' added Bob with a secret smile.

The telephone bell brought the conversation to an end, so Sally didn't see the satisfied expression on her father's face. 'Reckon it'll happen sooner than you think,' he murmured.

But there was a frown on Sally's face as she returned from her lengthy talk with Brad. 'What's he up to now?' she wondered aloud. 'We were going to meet the gang on Saturday night in Libchester. I'm longing to show him off to them, but he's asked me to postpone it until Sunday. We won't be going over to Libchester until Saturday as Brad has no idea how late he'll get back from London tomorrow.'

She was still puzzling over Brad's behaviour when she went to bed.

In the end it wasn't until Saturday afternoon that Brad and Sally arrived at the flat in Libchester. The late autumn afternoon was already fading into evening as they put away food and clothes. Once Brad was satisfied there were no more possible distractions to interrupt them, he drew Sally down onto the settee and took her in his arms. His first tender kiss soon deepened to tell her of his need and love.

'I've waited two long days for that, my darling,' he murmured into her hair as he cuddled her close. 'You smell lovely, and feel lovely and taste lovely, my lovely Sally.' He nuzzled into the soft skin of her neck sending shivers of pleasure through Sally's body. 'Did you miss me?'

'Of course I missed you, you daft man,' Sally laughed up at him. Her face became more serious. 'I miss you all the time, Brad. I never knew one person could so quickly become a part of my life, my thoughts, my very being. I'm only half alive when you're not with me. It's funny now when I look back at my life. I was upset when Laurence left, of course, but I think now it was more hurt pride than anything else. By the time you came along I was very content with my lot, happy the children were recovered and glad to be able to help Dad. I had my concerns in the village and friends all around me. I thought I was happy, but I didn't know what happiness was until you made me fall in love with you.'

'Made you? That sounds as if you didn't want to.'

'I certainly wasn't ready to fall in love. It was the furthest thing from my mind or intentions at that time. But I couldn't help myself. You crept up on me and before I knew it, there you were, deep in my heart, settled in for good.'

'I know what you mean,' Brad smiled ruefully. 'I had no idea this cheeky little urchin, who turned into a sexy woman almost overnight, would be the argumentative, tender-hearted, opinionated, sometime fire-cracker who would get under my guard and teach me how to love. For that I thank you, my darling. My mother would thank you too if she were here, because all she ever wanted was my happiness. You have given me all the love and happiness I need to fill my life and I'm sure you intend to argue with

me enough to keep me from becoming a dictator again.'
He punctuated his last sentence with kisses dabbed all over
Sally's face until she was laughing helplessly.

Then Brad drew away from her so he could turn her to
face him.

'My darling, you'll never know how much I love you.
My love is so deep, so boundless, it can't be measured. I
understand, now, those words of the love songs I thought
were so silly. How deep is the ocean, how high is the sky?
That's exactly what I mean. It's immeasurable. My
darling, please let me spend the rest of my life trying to
make you happy. Sally, will you marry me?'

Sally's eyes were like stars. Her heart swelled till she
couldn't breathe. Her lips trembled. For a moment all she
could do was to nod her head. Then her breath came back.

'Yes! Oh, yes. Oh, yes. Please. Yes, I love you so
much, Brad.'

She threw her arms around his neck and held up her
face for his lips. They sealed their union with a kiss so
deep all sense was lost. The love in each heart passed from
one to the other to become one flaring emotion. As they
at last drew apart, they were awed by its force. Brad took
a shaky breath and slipped his hand into his pocket to
withdraw a small jeweller's box. Flipping open the lid he
offered it for Sally's inspection.

'If you don't like it, just say what you want and I'll
have another made. The diamond is because it's the most
precious stone in the world for the most precious woman
in my life. The man offered me all sorts of other gems to
set it off, but nothing seemed right until he brought out the
topazes. I see that tawny gold in the lights in your hair and
the golden flecks in your eyes. It's the colour of the leaves
now on your beloved trees and it called to me. I'm Sally's
colour. Am I mad?'

Sally shook her head, speechless with gratitude for Brad's tender thoughtfulness. He hadn't splashed out his millions on the biggest, most expensive engagement ring in the shop, but chosen the humble topaz because of its meaning for them both. Not that he'd stinted on the diamond.

'I love you, Sally Fletcher,' he said as he pushed the ring onto her finger and set it in place with a kiss.

'It fits!'

Sally's surprise brought a smile to Brad's face. 'Thanks to a bit of conspiracy with Bob,' he explained. 'He lent me a ring of your mother's which he knows will fit you on either hand and also a pair of gloves.'

'Which you had to have back by Sunday for me to wear to church,' Sally finished, remembering an overheard telephone call. 'Wow!' she exclaimed as she admired the ring on her finger, turning it this way and that until the reflected light threw rainbows round the room from the perfect facets of the central diamond. On either side the topazes glowed with the same colours of Autumn which decked the trees in the garden beyond the window.

'I love my ring, Brad. I wouldn't change a thing about it and I love you too for giving it to me. You've made me so happy.'

'I have another present for you. I think this might make you even happier.'

'Impossible.'

'We'll see.' He pulled an envelope out of his other pocket and placed it in Sally's hands.

'What is it?'

'Open it and find out,' Brad suggested with a smile.

Wonderingly Sally slit open the envelope, stopping to admire the way her ring sparkled as she moved her hands. She pulled out a stiff document, unfolded it and read the contents half-way through. Then she blinked, looked at Brad in disbelief and went back to the beginning to start again and read more slowly.

'It's a Deed of Gift,' she said in disbelief. 'You're giving me Home Park, for ever. Oh, Brad. Does this mean you're going to change the development?'

'I guess I'll have to now that Home Park doesn't belong to me,' he grinned.

'Oh, Brad. Oh, my darling. I don't know what to say.'

'Say, thank you very much, Brad.'

'Thank you very, very much, my darling, Brad. You know why I didn't want you to chop down the trees, don't you?'

'Tell me.'

'I want our children to run and play among those trees, just as I did. I want us to have picnics and games with them. I want to teach our children to know and love Nature they way I was taught to do.'

'That'll definitely be your department. The teaching, I mean. You know how clueless I am.'

'Then you can be a pupil too Mr Big Businessman.'

Brad caught her in his arms again. 'I love it when you tease me. No-one has ever done that before.'

'You'd better get used to it then. I don't intend to stop.'

'How soon can we be married? I'd like to conceive the first of these children in the shade of a huge oak tree, but I don't think I can wait until Summer before making you my bride.'

'I'll marry you as soon as you like. I can't bear this ban on lovemaking you've placed on us. Brad what are you doing?'

He swept her up into his arms and carried her into the bedroom, tumbling with her onto the wide double bed.

'I said no love-making until my ring was on your finger,' he smiled wickedly. 'I didn't say which ring.'

He laughed down into her eyes as he gently began to undo the buttons of her blouse. His grey eyes darkened with passion as he felt her respond to his touch. Their lips met in welcome and the age-old rhythm of love began again.

THE END

Acknowledgements

Once more I have so many people to thank, for background information, inspiration and support along the way in the writing of this book.

My friends in the Ulverston Writers are ever ready with their helpful critiques as the work progresses on the first draft. Then I put the book away and concentrate on other things. When I eventually come back to it, it is with a fresh mind.

At this stage I know I can rely on my two faithful proof-readers Jeannie French and Peggy Savage for their eagle-eyed spotting of typos and other mistakes while I tighten up the story.

My books would never be completed without my friend and talented manipulator of technology, Graham Troth. To him I owe the amazing book covers he creates for me

To all the above and many more for odd snippets of unconscious inspiration I offer my enormous gratitude.

And of course, always my husband, Alick, for his patience and constant support.

Huge appreciation to you all

Gillian

www.ingramcontent.com/pod-product-compliance
Lightning Source LLC
Chambersburg PA
CBHW060502290526
45791CB00001B/226